The Tram Western S

GW00722492

(Networks Edition)

This book, the fourteenth in our regional series, and the second of two on Scotland, is based on Chapter 12 of *Great British Tramway Networks* by W.H.Bett and J.C.Gillham published in its fourth edition in 1962 and long out of print. We trace the history of those tramways which operated in Western Scotland from Carstairs in the south-east to Balloch in the north and Rothesay on the Isle of Bute well to the west.

There were formerly ten electric tramway systems, and a number of light railways, of which the most important, and the hub of the network, was Glasgow. At one time the city's tramcars could be seen as far afield as Airdrie in Lanarkshire, Kilbarchan in Renfrewshire, and Dalmuir West in Dumbartonshire, respectively 12, 13 and 8 miles from the city centre. By changing cars at Dalmuir West, it was possible from 1908 to 1928 to reach the shores of Loch Lomond twenty miles to the north-west, or by way of Cambuslang or Uddingston to travel to Newmains or Larkhall, 17 or 14 miles to the south-east of the city centre. Several commercial firms in Glasgow employed their own electric locomotives for hauling railway wagons over the Corporation tramways, the last being a shipyard in the Govan area.

An unusual feature of all the systems centred on Glasgow was the track gauge adopted, which, right from the earliest horse days, was 4ft.7¾in. throughout, as it was intended to run railway wagons on the tram track and give through goods services. The depth of the flange of a railway wheel is greater than the depth of the groove in a tram rail, and so the railway wagons had to run on the flanges of their wheels, instead of on their tyres, and the taper of the flanges necessitated a reduction of gauge of ¾ inch.

Our geographical sequence is from Carstairs, following the Clyde valley downstream through Motherwell and Glasgow to Dumbarton and Greenock, on either side of the estuary, across to Rothesay, and then back along the coast, inland to Kilmarnock and out again to Ayr, some 35 miles west of our starting point, although we will have covered almost one hundred by our route. We will complete the story with a look at some minor lines and the Glasgow Subway.

Carstairs House

The visitor from the south following the traditional west coast railway route would first come to Carstairs, where the lines to Edinburgh and Glasgow diverge. This was the site of Scotland's earliest electric tramway, a 2ft. 6in. gauge line with side-conductor rail, linking the station with Carstairs House, just over one mile to the south-west. It was built by

Cover. **Maryhill terminus in April 1960 with Cunarder 1382 and Coronation 1244 waiting to cross over and depart for Ballieston. Unfortunately it can no longer continue ahead to Milngavie, the service having been cutback to Maryhill on 3 November 1956.** *(R. J. S. Wiseman)*

Back cover

Above **Glasgow 1068 restored to open-top condition as Paisley 68 is seen at the Glasgow Garden Festival with the River Clyde as a background. 3 September 1988.** *(G. R. Tribe)*

Below **Glasgow Hex-dash Standard 206 at Bishopbriggs Terminus. April 1960.** *(R. J. S. Wiseman)*

Joseph Monteith and opened in 1889, with power obtained from a nearby waterfall, but electric operation appears to have ceased by 1896, and horses were then used until about 1925 to transport coal and other goods from the station to the house. The locally-built single-deck four-wheeled car had an eight horse power motor and seated six passengers. There were also two unpowered luggage vans.

The Carstairs tram approaches the terminus at Carstairs House. Note the conductor rails. The driver has his right hand on the controller, his left on the brake.

(Royal Scottish Museum

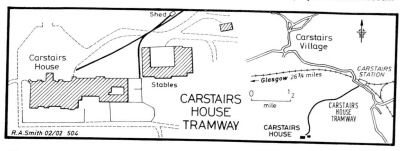

Motherwell

Ten miles to the north-west of Carstairs we reach Newmains, the outer terminus of a lengthy line, via Wishaw, to Motherwell in the heart of the Lanarkshire industrial area, its prosperity based on coal and high-grade iron ore. These raw materials, together with easy access to the ports of the Clyde, resulted in the development of steel, and a wide range of engineering industries, including from 1880 the building of more than 50,000 railway wagons, and later tramcars, at Motherwell. Here Hurst Nelson & Co., Ltd. built over 600 complete cars and well over 1,200 bodies between 1899 and 1934, two-thirds of them destined for the London County Council Tramways.

Lanarkshire and Glasgow trams met at Uddingston Cross in 1907, but the rails were never joined, although the Lanarkshire tracks were later continued round the corner to Bellshill and Holytown. *(South Lanarkshire Council*

Although the Glasgow, Bothwell, Hamilton and Wishaw Tramways Act of 1872 authorised tramways from Glasgow to these three towns and also Motherwell, the district had to wait another thirty years for a tramway. A proposed Hamilton, Motherwell and Wishaw Light Railway of 1898 was not authorised, and it was not until 1900 that the Hamilton, Motherwell and Wishaw Tramways Act received the Royal Assent, and even then construction, to the 4ft.7¾in gauge, did not begin until June 1902.

The Hamilton, Motherwell and Wishaw Light Railways Company, Ltd. in which The British Thomson-Houston Company had an interest, opened the tramway linking these towns on 22 July 1903 following the official inspection the previous day. The Company had adopted the simpler Lanarkshire Tramways Company title earlier in 1903, and proceeded to expand its tramway system – to Larkhall in 1905, Cambuslang in 1907, Uddingston via Bothwell also Wishaw to Newmains in 1909, and finally Motherwell to New Stevenston in 1911. To complete the system the Lanarkshire County Council obtained an Act in 1912, under which the authorised lines from Uddingston to New Stevenston via Bellshill, and the Holytown branch, were opened in 1913-14 and worked by the Company on lease, until purchased in 1921. However, the authorised link from Glasgow's Uddingston tramway near Broomhouse to Bellshill was not built. An earlier proposed Company extension from Larkhall to Garrion Bridge was not authorised, and nothing came of a proposal by Hamilton Town Council for a tramway south to Low Waters at Eddlewood Bridge.

The result was a large system of 28½ route miles, unfortunately mainly single track with passing loops (13½ miles), and worked by 76 double-deck, single-truck cars. Even though new cars were obtained and others rebuilt to modern standards as late as 1925, sadly the proposal to build 12 high-speed bogie cars was shelved, though it is doubtful if they would have saved the system. The trams could not survive the intense motor bus competition and were abandoned in the Winter of 1930-31, after which the Lanarkshire, with its associated Central SMT Co., Ltd., became and remained Scotland's fourth-largest bus company for almost fifty years.

Two Glasgow Standard cars, Nos. 278 and 872, on the Airdrie-Coatbridge local service pass at Dundyvan Road, Coatbridge, on 8 August 1953. *(R. J. S. Wiseman)*

Airdrie

Airdrie, together with Coatbridge some two miles to the west, developed rapidly as centres of the iron industry following the opening of the Monklands Canal in 1790. Many tramway schemes were proposed; among the earliest, in 1872, were the Glasgow and Monklands Tramways Company, and the Glasgow, Coatbridge and Airdrie Tramways Company. The proposed lines would have linked both towns with Glasgow, but the Bills were dismissed.

In 1896 the Electric Construction Company Ltd., of Wolverhampton, proposed a double-track line of 3½ miles from Langloan, west of Coatbridge, to Airdrie, but nothing came of this or other schemes, until the British Electric Traction Company applied in 1898 for a 3ft. 6in. gauge Coatbridge & Airdrie Light Railway under the new 1896 Act. This was approved provided the gauge was altered to 4ft.8½in, but in 1899 was finally rejected on the grounds that, although greatly needed, it was entirely in an urban area and must therefore go to Parliament as a tramway and could not be a light railway. The local electricity company, Scottish House-to-House Electricity Supply Co. Ltd. (successors to the New General Traction Co. Ltd.), obtained the Airdrie & Coatbridge Tramways Act in 1900, with powers to build the line as a tramway. The BET purchased this company in 1903 and its powers to build a tramway, now of 4ft.7¾in. gauge, from Langloan through Coatbridge to Clarkston, almost a mile beyond Airdrie. However, this latter section, and a half-mile branch in Coatbridge along Sunnyside Road, were never built.

Public service commenced on Monday 8 February 1904 after an official ceremony the previous Friday. The original Coatbridge terminus at Kirkwood Street, Langloan, was extended to Woodside Street on 16 August 1905, and some sections of track were doubled in 1907 and 1913. Brush supplied 15 extended canopy, single-truck cars, one of which, No.14, was fitted with a top cover. Two others, Nos. 13 and 15, received locally-built covers.

Proposals to link the Airdrie tramway with that of Glasgow at Baillieston, reached from the city in 1906, were finalised in 1914, but the outbreak of the Great War delayed its construction for seven years. The Airdrie tramway was purchased by the two Burghs on 1 October 1920, and then sold to Glasgow Corporation who took over the line on 1 January 1922. The new 2¼ mile reserved-track light railway linking Coatbridge at Langloan with Glasgow at Baillieston was opened on 30 December 1923, and six months later the original tramway was closed for reconstruction. It was rebuilt with double track throughout, and re-opened for public service on 23 May 1925 with lengthy through services, 20 miles to Paisley, and, some months later, 16 miles to Anniesland. This latter service was extended one mile to Knightswood on 30 November 1926.

The Airdrie services continued to operate successfully, latterly to Anderston Cross and Maryhill, until 1956 when, under a new agreement with local bus companies, they were cut back to the city boundary at Baillieston. The last tram left Airdrie for the ex-company depot at Jackson Street, Airdrie, in the early hours of 4 November 1956.

Union Street, Glasgow, from the Argyle Street intersection. Glasgow Standard 748 on a Giffnock service is being followed by a Coronation on service 24 to Langside. 10 August 1953.
(R. J. S. Wiseman

Glasgow

The dredging and improvements of the River Clyde during the nineteenth century were the principal factors in the growth of Glasgow as a major port and industrial centre for central Scotland. The building of the Monkland, and Forth & Clyde canals, and later railways, greatly assisted this development, with shipbuilding the dominant industry.

A tramway for the city was first proposed by G.F. Train in 1860, but this did not progress, and it was not until 1869 that further progress was made. Two rival London syndicates promoted Bills in Parliament; they were both opposed by Glasgow Corporation, but agreement was eventually reached between the parties. The resulting

Was the Union Street — Argyle Street crossing the exact centre of Glasgow? In this view No. 673 from Cambuslang is heading down Argyle Street to Partick and Anniesland, while in the background Coronations and Cunarders are on north-south services via Renfield Street and Eglinton Street. 7 April 1958. *(R. J. S. Wiseman*

Glasgow Street Tramways Act of 1870 enabled the Corporation to construct tramways within the city, which were then leased to the Glasgow Tramway & Omnibus Company Limited for 23 years from 1 July 1871. Although the first tracks were laid in Great Western Road to standard gauge, they were never used and the first horse tram ran on 4ft. 7¾in gauge tracks on 19 August 1872 from St. Georges Cross to Eglinton Toll, and the Company within a few years was operating a fleet of 233 cars over 25 miles of track.

When the time for compulsory municipalisation came on 1 July 1894 the Company refused to sell out to the Corporation, with whom it had always quarrelled, so on 30 June 1894 its trams ran for the last time within the city. Glasgow Corporation took over the next morning with a fleet of brand new trams and 3000 fresh horses operating out of new stables and depots.

The Corporation was one of the pioneers of electric traction, and the first line, from Mitchell Street to Springburn, was opened on 13 October 1898. Electrification proceeded apace, and 385 horse trams had been replaced when the last few were withdrawn from the Tollcross extension on 14 April 1902. None of the trams were over eight years old and it is not surprising that 120 were rebuilt for electric traction.

Routes radiated in all directions from the city centre in a very close mesh, east-west on Argyle and Sauchiehall Streets and north-south on Hope, Renfield, West Nile and High Streets. The system continued to develop with lines extending well beyond the city boundary, out to Clydebank, Renfrew, Rouken Glen, Clarkston, Rutherglen, Uddingston, Millerston and Bishopbriggs. The last extension of note, 3½ miles, was from Maryhill to Milngavie in 1934. There were further short extensions in 1949, to Carnwadric and from Knightswood along the Great Western Road to Blairdardie. There were plans to extend this further towards Duntocher, the terminus of a branch from Clydebank, but the Cloberhill opening bridge over the Forth and Clyde Canal at Blairdardie was not rebuilt at that time.

9

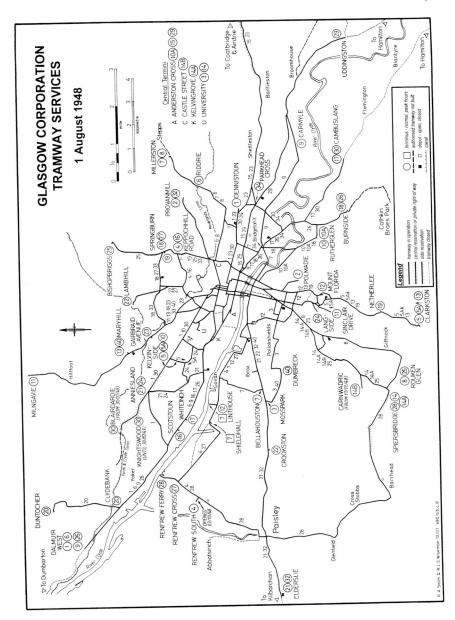

GLASGOW CORPORATION
TRAMWAY SERVICES

1 August 1948

R. A. Smith & R. J. S. Wiseman 12/01 490/a,b,c,d

Unlike most English cities, the Glasgow Corporation owned instead of leasing, the lines beyond its boundaries, and although some of the outside areas were later incorporated into the enlarged city boundaries Glasgow did at one time own tramways in the Burghs of Rutherglen, Pollokshaws, Govan, Partick, Milngavie, Clydebank, and Renfrew, with extensive sections in the counties of Lanark, Renfrew and Dumbarton, all these in addition to the lines of the Airdrie and Paisley companies which it later took over.

There were formerly 14 car depots within the city, but five of these were later replaced by extensions to the others, so that, together with the acquired depots in Coatbridge and Elderslie, the Corporation eventually owned eleven. It also owned a magnificent power station at Pinkston which for some time was the only survivor still owned by British tram or trolleybus undertakings outside London. Glasgow's car-building and overhaul works at Coplawhill were one of the finest in the country, and all save 130 of the city's new trams were built there. On closure it housed the museum fleet of trams until the new Museum of Transport at Kelvingrove was opened in April 1988.

Although the system opened with 21 single-deck 'Room & Kitchen' bogie cars the mainstay of the fleet was the famous Glasgow Standard, a double-deck single-truck car, totalling 1005 units, which was developed from uncanopied, open-top in 1899 to all-enclosed in 1923. The majority of the older cars were rebuilt enclosed, and speeded-up, and a few served the city for over sixty years. Some, including ex-Paisley cars, were cut down to single-deck for the Clydebank-Duntocher service. In 1938, to serve the Empire Exhibition at Mosspark a fleet of new bogie 'Coronation' cars was introduced, possibly the finest doubledeck cars ever built. They were followed in 1948 by a modified version, the 'Cunarder'. The last new cars to be built were six of the Coronation type on ex-Liverpool bogies in 1954.

A peculiarity of Glasgow trams not seen elsewhere in this country after the horse era, except in Aberdeen, was the distinguishing of different services by painting the upper-deck panels in different colours. Although there were only five such colours (red, green, blue, yellow and white) they were so arranged that, except in a few inner streets, no two

The renewal of the tram tracks on the Renfrew Road with new foundations during the Autumn of 1954 did not delay the service. Cunarder 1377 passed on its way to Renfrew on 10 September 1954.
(R. J. S. Wiseman

services of the same colour traversed the same roads. The colours had disappeared by 1952 and all top decks became pale green. Route numbers were introduced in 1924, but later dropped, and then revived again in 1938 for the benefit of visitors to the Exhibition.

The Glasgow tramways were maintained to the highest standards with major track renewals as late as 1954, long sections of the Renfrew Road, and the Renfield Street-Sauchiehall Street junctions, being replaced. The system of 134¾ route miles was all double track except for a short section of ex-Paisley tramway between Glenfield and Cross Stobs which was abandoned in 1949. Another feature was the extensive use of sidings on which short-working cars could reverse or lay over without fouling cars on through services.

In 1949 trolleybuses replaced the trams on the Polmadie-Provanmill service via the High Street, the site of the original settlement on its hill above the flood plain of the Clyde. The services to Clarkston followed in 1953, but there was no general abandonment plan, and in fact the general manager, Mr. E.R.L. Fitzpayne, had drawn up a scheme in 1948 to modernise the tramways and to introduce high-speed single-deck trams to serve them. His views, alas, did not prevail, and the trams were abandoned over a period of seven years, starting with the Paisley services in 1956 and culminating with the eleven-mile route from Auchenshuggle to Dalmuir West in September 1962.

In 1995 Strathclyde Regional Council drew up plans for a new tramway system using redundant railway rights-of-way and city centre streets from Maryhill to Easterhouse, well to the east of the erstwhile terminus at Dennistoun. These plans were rejected in 1996, but these or similar schemes may yet come to pass at some time in the future.

This view is typical of the Glasgow urban scene in the l900's. No. 370 is seen heading west towards Linthouse terminus. The car was built unvestibuled with a balcony top cover, and was scrapped in November 1960 in its final enclosed condition.
(Herald Series, Courtesy National Tramway Museum

Govan

Downstream from Glasgow, Govan developed as a shipbuilding centre with major yards at Linthouse, and was an independent Burgh until 1912. The first Bill of the Vale of Clyde Tramways Co., Ltd. was thrown out of Parliament in 1870, but the second was passed in 1871. This authorised two separate systems, one connecting Greenock with Port Glasgow, and one in Govan. The latter was from Paisley Road Toll, where connection was made with the Glasgow system, to Govan Cross. A through service worked by the Glasgow Tramway & Omnibus Company from St.Vincent Place to Govan Station opened on 1 January 1873, but this lasted only until early in 1875 when the service was curtailed to Paisley Road Toll and passengers had to change. The next Vale of Clyde Tramways Act, in 1876, was the first in the United Kingdom to authorise the use of mechanical traction on a street tramway, and steam traction was introduced on 20 August 1877 with ten Hughes engines. These were replaced in 1881 by Kitson machines. In addition the Scott-Moncrieff Pneumatic car, an ex-Edinburgh car converted to compressed-air traction, ran experimentally on the Govan Road, probably in 1875, and for a time in 1877. The service was extended to Linthouse in 1884 over tracks which had only been used up to that time for moving railway wagons from Govan Goods Yard to the shipyards at Linthouse.

The tramway was taken over by the Govan Burgh in 1893 and leased to the G.T & O Company, and steam traction gave way to horses. In the meantime, on 18 July 1879, the Glasgow & Ibrox Tramway Company had opened a line from The Toll for a mile along the Paisley Road towards Ibrox Station which it never reached. This line was operated by four Eades reversible-type tramcars. Govan Burgh also took over this line, and leased it to the G.T.& O., who, from 18 May 1894, ran a through service into Glasgow. When Glasgow Corporation took over the city lines in 1894 the G.T.& O. continued to work the lines in Govan with its own horse cars until 11 November 1896 when Glasgow took over the lease. Glasgow's electric cars first ran to Linthouse on 10 August 1901, and to Ibrox, extended to Halfway House, a week later.

Paisley

In due course the Ibrox route was extended along Paisley Road West through Crookston, and on to Hawkhead Road, half a mile inside the Paisley boundary. this latter section opening on 25 November 1903. At this point it connected with the Paisley system.

Paisley developed around its abbey, and later industrially, with first weaving, and later cotton thread manufacture. Horse tramways were introduced on 30 December 1885 by the Paisley Tramways Company, and services eventually extended from Hawkhead Road through Paisley to Thomas Street, near Ferguslie Mills. Double-deck and single-deck cars were used, and an experiment with a battery-equipped car took place in 1887.

Proposals for electric traction first came in 1898 when the British Electric Traction Company promoted the Paisley Light Railway Order. This was opposed by Glasgow and other councils and did not proceed, and it was not until 1901 that the Paisley District Tramways Act, promoted by William Murphy, chairman of the Dublin United and other companies, was passed. The Paisley District Tramways Company electric system was almost the only company one to be sanctioned by Parliament in spite of severe opposition from the local authority which wanted to build one of its own.

Construction of the new electric system did not start until late in 1903, and the first section, from Paisley Cross to Hawkhead Road, opened on 13 June 1904. This service was discontinued on 20 March 1905 when Glasgow Corporation took over and ran through services from the city to Paisley Cross.

Paisley Tramways Company horse car No. 36 of 1890 is posed at the East End terminus at Hawkhead Road. *(Courtesy National Tramway Museum*

An extensive system totalling 18¼ miles, centred on Paisley Cross, was built up, with lengthy lines out to Renfrew Ferry, Johnstone, extended to Kilbarchan in 1906, and to Potterhill, extended to Barrhead, also in 1906, and finally to Spiersbridge in 1910 where it met the Rouken Glen via Pollokshaws tramway of Glasgow Corporation. Here the Company opened a tea room and other amenities which were a popular attraction in the summer. Although the short branch to Abbotsinch was built those to the Racecourse and Meikleriggs, however, were not.

The Company, together with its depot at Elderslie and fleet of 68 four-wheel double-deck cars, was purchased by Glasgow Corporation in 1923, and as a result, two years later in 1925, the Renfrew Ferry -Paisley- Spiersbridge service was extended through Glasgow to Hillfoot, beyond Maryhill. When this line was extended to Milngavie on 7 October 1934 it become the longest tram route in Great Britain with a journey time of two hours for the 22.72 miles, costing 2½d (approx 1p). Services were also introduced from Ferguslie Mills through Paisley and Glasgow city centre, alternatively to Uddingston and Airdrie, 15.83 and 20.08 miles respectively, and the latter a journey time of 105 minutes. Another connection with the Glasgow system was installed at Renfrew Cross in 1932 and Glasgow services through Govan were extended to Porterfield Road (Renfrew South) and later to Paisley North. The short Abbotsinch route, and Kilbarchan line beyond Ferguslie Mllls (Elderslle), were closed in 1932-3.

In 1943 services were revised and long distance Paisley services shortened, those from Paisley running through to Anniesland or Provanmill, and that from Renfrew Ferry to Milngavie being split, with Ferry cars running only to Spiersbridge as in Company days. In 1949 the single-track section between Glenfield and Cross Stobs was closed, and the University-Spiersbridge service was extended through Barrhead to Cross Stobs.

The remains of the Paisley system, except for the two sections closed in 1932-33, Cross Stobs to Arden closed on 29 September 1956 and the short section from Spiersbridge to Arden which closed on 1 November 1959, closed on 12 May 1957, and a number of local bus companies which had competed with the trams over the years, took over, and now compete locally with the electric train services extending beyond Paisley via Johnstone to Ayr and Largs.

The Paisley Company's terminus at Renfrew Ferry attracted many passengers from the far side of the river, and numerous circular trips were possible, the best example being from Glasgow via Pollokshaws, Barrhead, Paisley, and Renfrew Ferry, across the Clyde to Yoker, and thence back to Glasgow.

Paisley District trams ran from Renfrew Ferry to Spiersbridge; Glasgow extended the service across the city centre to Milngavie, almost two hours away. This was cut back to Spiersbridge in 1943, and to Glenfield in 1949 when the country section was abandoned. Cunarder No. 1307 is seen at Cross Stobs on 5 August 1956.
(R. J. S. Wiseman

Dumbarton

The Glasgow Corporation line extending through Partick and Yoker to Clydebank and Dalmuir West, terminated end-on with the tracks of the inter-urban line to Dumbarton, Jamestown, and Balloch on the shores of Loch Lomond. The volcanic rock, 240 feet (73m) high, on which Dumbarton Castle stands, dominates the low-lying ground where the river Leven, flowing from Loch Lomond, enters the Clyde. Around its castle Dumbarton grew, with shipbuilding its major industry.

The earliest tramway proposal was in 1900 when a syndicate headed by William Murphy promoted the Glasgow District Tramways Bill for a line from Scotstoun (Glasgow) through Clydebank to Balloch, but it failed to obtain the approval of the local authorities and only the lines in Renfrew and Paisley went ahead. The next proposal came from Crompton & Co., Ltd. of Chelmsford, Essex, who owned the Electric Supply Corporation Limited, which in turn owned 18 electric supply undertakings, mainly in Eastern Scotland and south-west England. The Dumbarton Tramways Order was obtained

A Glasgow tram first crossed the Dalmuir Canal bridge on 10 February 1915, and the last, No. 1282, on 6 September 1962. Here, Kilmarnock Bogie, No.1094, with screens set for the return to Auchenshuggle, is heading to Dalmuir West. *(R. J. S. Wiseman*

in 1904, and on 20 February 1907 the Electric Supply Corporation opened its only electric tramway. This was three short routes, to Dalreoch, Dumbuck and Barloan Toll, in total only 2¼ miles, and worked by six double-deck open-balcony cars from Brush.

The Electric Supply Corporation Ltd. obtained the Dumbartonshire Tramways Confirmation Order on 21 December 1906, and in 1907 these powers were transferred to the Dumbarton Burgh and County Tramways Co., Ltd., which purchased the tramways within the Burgh, and was also a subsidiary of the Electric Supply Corporation.

Construction of 10¼ miles of new County extensions started early in 1908 and they were opened in stages. The Dalreoch route was extended through Renton to Alexandria in May, and then along the Luss Road almost to the shores of Loch Lomond at Balloch Railway Station. Meanwhile the line from Dumbuck had been extended through Bowling and Old Kilpatrick to the Clydebank boundary at Dalmuir West, and a through service from the canal bridge to Balloch started on 25 June 1908. The Glasgow Corporation trams at that time terminated at Dalmuir Canal Bridge, and the 'County' trams ran over 601 yards of Glasgow-owned track in Clydebank to the Burgh boundary at Dalmuir West. The canal bridge was rebuilt in 1914 and re-opened on 10 February 1915, and Corporation trams then ran through to Dalmuir West from 11 November in place of the 'County' ones. Twenty standard 'Preston' three-window, extended-canopy, open-top cars were obtained for the new Balloch through service, and 14 were in action on the first day. In due course the fleet totalled 32 cars.

At Alexandria a branch line to Jamestown via Bonhill was built during 1908, but its opening was delayed until 24 February 1909 because the County would not allow the roadway under a railway bridge in Alexandria to be lowered. As a result converted ex-Glasgow open-top horse trams with the upper decks closed off were used on the local Jamestown service.

The extended Dunbartonshire tramways were laid for the most part as single line with loops along narrow country lanes, but in the 1920's the trams were unable to compete, despite cheap weekend fares, with the bus 'free-for-all' along the road to the Loch. The trams ran for the last time on 3 March 1928, and the Company went into liquidation.

Through services to Glasgow were never established, but plans had been drawn up in 1914 for a new direct road, including a reserved track tramway, from Anniesland, Glasgow, to Bowling, together with thoughts of an extension through Bonhill to the Loch. When the road was eventually built the Glasgow tramway was first extended to Knightswood and later, on 31 July 1949, to Blairdardie, but not onwards towards Duntocher as intended 34 years earlier.

Glasgow Standard 760, probably a shipyard extra, is seen at Dalmuir West terminus on 8 August 1953. Until 3 March 1928 passengers could change on to a 'County' car for Dumbarton and Loch Lomond. *(R. J. S. Wiseman*

Greenock

On the south bank of the Clyde opposite Dumbarton, Greenock also developed shipbuilding industries, together with sugar refining and others based on imported raw materials. The town developed along the flat coastal plain alongside the river and eventually the built-up area extended downstream to Gourock and upstream to Port Glasgow.

The first tramway opened on 7 July 1873 from Greenock to Gourock. It was operated on lease from the Burgh Council by the Vale of Clyde Tramways Company, which was already active in Govan. It was horse operated although a Dickenson steam tram ran experimentally in 1877. The Greenock and Port Glasgow Tramways Company was formed in 1887 by an Act of 8 August to connect the two towns, and their line opened on 29 November 1889, again with horse traction. When the Vale of Clyde lease of the earlier line expired in 1894 the G & PG Company took it over, and ran both as a unified system.

The Company came into the British Electric Traction group in May 1900, and the lines were re-opened with electric traction on 3 October 1901 and through services established

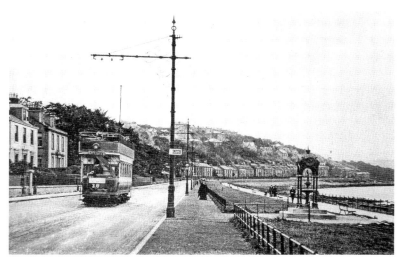

No.18, one of the large Brush Maximum-traction cars in the Greenock fleet, is heading towards the Ashton terminus. Note the fare stage.sign. *(Courtesy Roy Brook)*

along the solitary 7½ mile route with 30 very large double-deck bogie cars which seated 74 passengers. These were later augmented by a further twelve not quite so large. The tramway followed the flat river plain all the way, extensions away from the river being prevented by the steep hills rising immediately behind the three towns.

The tramway prospered initially, but as elsewhere, with increasing competition, and need for the extensive renewal of track and rolling stock, the system became unprofitable. Although some track renewals were carried out and four cars were top-covered, the Company did not wish to renew the lease and the tramway closed on 15 July 1929. The Company was absorbed into the Scottish Motor Traction Group in 1931, but it remained in existence until 1951 with a fleet of over 100 buses.

Rothesay

Continuing downstream along the estuary of the Clyde either by rail to Wemyss Bay for a ferry connection, or by steamer from Glasgow, we arrive at Rothesay on the Isle of Bute, some seven miles west of the mainland. Initially a fishing town, it has developed as a holiday resort for Glasgow and the surrounding industrial area.

The Rothesay Tramways Company Ltd. was incorporated on 20 December 1879 and obtained the Rothesay Tramways Order in 1880. This authorised a little over two miles of four-foot gauge tramway from Guildford Square, close by Rothesay Pier, to Port Bannatyne, It opened on 1 June 1882 with 12 single-deck horse cars, eight open with canvas roofs, and four closed ones, supplied by the Saville Street Foundry & Engineering Company of Sheffield. Further open cars were built locally.

The British Electric Traction Company Ltd. proposed electric traction in 1897, and by 1901 had obtained control of the Company, (there were only three BET companies in Scotland), and an Act in 1900 to work the line by mechanical power. The horse trams ceased running on 2 March 1902, and the line was reconstructed double-track throughout to the narrower 3ft. 6in. gauge. Horse cars resumed service on the 3ft. 6in. gauge tracks

Beflagged Rothesay open toastrack No. 11 or 12 awaits passengers from the steamers at Rothesay terminus. *(M. J. O'Connor, National Tramway Museum)*

on 17 May 1902 and operated until the line re-opened with electric traction on 19 August 1902, six days after the formal inauguration. In the meantime the Company had obtained powers to extend the line, on private right-of-way, across the island to Ettrick Bay, on which a speed of 25mph was authorised. This opened on 13 July 1905, but an extension in the opposite direction along the coast to Craigmore Pier, and a further short extension at Ettrick Bay, were not constructed.

The tramway followed the curve of Rothesay Bay, and beyond the picturesque harbour of Port Bannatyne went cross-country between the hills, with wide ranging views of sea and mountain, to the sands of Ettrick Bay. Unusually for a rural BET line the 4¾ miles of route were entirely double track.

The Company had a fleet of 20 long single-deck cars, mainly of the toastrack type, and these would be crowded during the Summer holiday season carrying visitors to the Bay, where the Company would lay on entertainments. There was also a small demi-car obtained from Greenock in 1916, which obtained a new open body in 1920.

The winter service was withdrawn from January 1931, and later in the same year control passed to the Scottish Motor Traction Company. The line closed at the end of the Summer season of 1936, but the Rothesay Tramways Company buses still carried the fleet name of 'Tramways' in large letters on their sides until 1950.

Ardrossan

Back on the mainland again at Wemyss Bay, a steam tramway of nine miles southwards to Largs and Fairlie was proposed in 1877, and in 1905 an electric line to Largs only, and partly on reserved track, was put forward, but as far as is known this proposal did not come before Parliament. Further south we reach West Kilbride, where the Scottish Electric Traction Company Ltd.'s offshoot, the Ardrossan, Salcoats & District Tramways Company, proposed 11½ miles of coastal tramway southwards from Portencross through Ardrossan, Saltcoats and Stevenston to the isolated dynamite works on Irvine Bay. The proposed line was single-track with passing places, and included sections of reserved track between the towns.

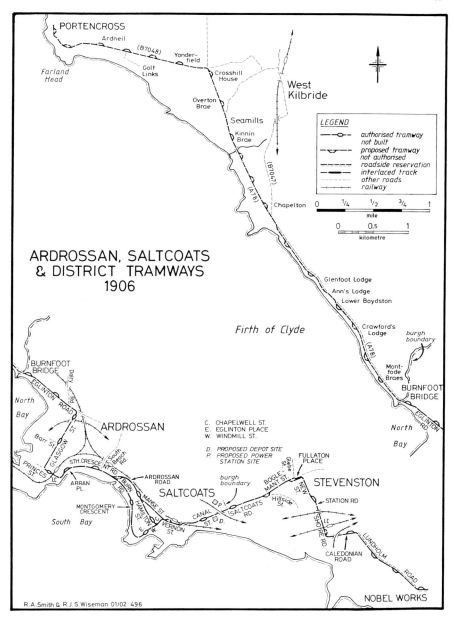

ARDROSSAN, SALTCOATS
& DISTRICT TRAMWAYS
1906

PORTENCROSS
Ardneil
(B7048)
Yonder-field
Golf Links
Farland Head
Crosshill House
Overton Brae
West Kilbride
Seamills
Kinnin Brae
(B7047)
(A78)
Chapelton

Firth of Clyde

Glenfoot Lodge
Ann's Lodge
Lower Boydston
Crawford's Lodge
burgh boundary
(A78)
Mont-fode Braes
BURNFOOT BRIDGE
EGLINTON RD.
North Bay

BURNFOOT BRIDGE
EGLINTON ROAD
Dalry Rd.
North Bay

ARDROSSAN
Barr St.
GLASGOW ST.
STH. CRESCENT RD.
South Beach Rd.
PRINCES ST.
LC
ARRAN PL.
ARDROSSAN ROAD
BURNS RD.
MANSE ST.
HAMILTON ST.
MONTGOMERY CRESCENT
South Bay
VERNON ST.
E
W

SALTCOATS
CANAL ST.
D.
P.
SALTCOATS RD.
burgh boundary
Hillside St.
BOGLE ST.
MANT ST.
Glebe St.
FULLATON PLACE
NEW ST.
STEVENSTON
STATION RD.
SHORE RD.
LC
CALEDONIAN ROAD
LUNDHOLM ROAD
NOBEL WORKS

C. CHAPELWELL ST.
E. EGLINTON PLACE
W. WINDMILL ST.

D. PROPOSED DEPOT SITE
P. PROPOSED POWER STATION SITE

LEGEND
○—○— authorised tramway not built
◁—▷ proposed tramway not authorised
---- roadside reservation
▬▬▬ interlaced track
- - - other roads
+—+—+ railway

0   ¼   ½   ¾   1
mile

0   0.5   1
kilometre

R.A.Smith & R.J.S.Wiseman 01/02 496

In the event the AS&DT Order Confirmation Act, which received the Royal Assent in December 1906, only authorised the 6¼ miles from Ardrossan Burgh northern boundary at Burnfoot Bridge south through the town and Saltcoats to the dynamite works. The tramway was never built, the Scottish Electric Traction Company being wound up in 1910, and although the Ardrossan and Saltcoats Electric Light & Power Company, Ltd., owned by Balfour Beatty, included tramways among its objectives, the Ardrossan tramway scheme was finally abandoned in 1914. This is not surprising, as the streets of Saltcoats and Stevenston were very narrow and, at Stevenston, a mile short of the terminus, passengers would have to have walked across the level crossing at the Glasgow & South Western Railway Station, as the tramway here was not authorised to carry passengers.

Kilmarnock No.10, bound for Hurlford, has just entered Duke Street.
(Raphael Tuck Card, courtesy National Tramway Museum

Kilmarnock

Some twelve miles inland from Ardrossan the Burgh of Kilmarnock, situated on the Ayrshire Coalfield, developed woollen and engineering industries. Among the latter was locomotive building , with Andrew Barclay, Dick Kerr, and the Glasgow & South Western Railway being prominent.

The Corporation obtained powers in 1901 to build a power station, and the British Electric Traction Company offered to lease the tramway if built. However Kilmarnock wished to run their own tramway, and to this end obtained the Kilmarnock Corporation Act in 1904. This authorised lines to Beansburn, Hurlford and Riccarton totalling a mere 4¼ miles. The gauge was the standard 4ft. 8½in., rare for Western Scotland, and there were 14 four-wheel, double-deck cars, all built by Hurst Nelson. One of them, No.12, was exhibited at the third Tramway and Light Railway Exhibition held in London in 1905. It later ran as the town's decorated car.

The Kilmarnock system had a very short life; it was too small to survive, and with expenditure exceeding receipts, and mining subsidence enhancing track maintenance costs, abandonment was only a matter of time. The Hurlford route closed in 1924 and the others failed to restart at the end of the general strike in May 1926. It thus became the first municipal electric tramway north of the border to cease operation. Replacement was by municipal motor buses, which were themselves replaced on 1 January 1932 by those of the Scottish Motor Traction Co., Ltd.

An Ayr balcony car is approaching the loop at Burns Cottage, Alloway, a traffic focus for Ayr trams. *(Commercial card, courtesy National Tramway Museum)*

Kilmarnock's name, however, lives on in that the Kilmarnock Engineering Company, successors to the Dick Kerr Britannia Works in 1919, built the maximum-traction bogies for Glasgow trams Nos.1091-1140, of which Nos.1100 and 1115 still exist in museums.

Ayr

The ancient Royal Burgh of Ayr lies twelve miles to the south-west of Kilmarnock, and was initially a port and trading centre, but by 1900 its main function was as a holiday resort thanks to a fine beach and connections with Robert Burns. His cottage at Alloway and the golf course at Prestwick attracted many tramway promoters, and in October 1883 the Ayr & District Tramways Company was formed to link the two attractions. The scheme was approved by Parliament in 1884, but although a prospectus was issued in 1886 the project was abandoned two years later. Next came an application in 1898 by the Drake and Gorham Electric Power & Traction Syndicate Ltd. for an Ayr, Prestwick and Monkton Light Railway. This line of 4¼ miles of 3ft.6in. gauge electric tramway, which would have linked Ayr with the villages of Prestwick and Monkton to the north, was rejected.

The Council however, like Kilmarnock, also wished to run its own tramway, and by the Ayr Burgh Act of 1899 obtained the necessary powers, and in September 1901 opened 6¼ miles of standard-gauge line (not 4ft.7¾in.) from the historic Burns Monument at Brig o'Doon in the south through the centre of the town to the popular holiday resort of Prestwick. There was also a short branch to the racecourse; this was only busy on race days and was served latterly by four single-deck demi-cars, Nos.25-28. These were converted from single-deck cars built by Brush in 1899 for the Oldham, Ashton and Hyde Tramways Company and bought from Manchester Corporation in 1922. The main fleet consisted of 17 open-top and six covered-top single-truck cars supplied by Hurst Nelson between 1901 and 1915. These included a special car which had been exhibited in London in 1902, three years earlier than that at Kilmarnock. This was a superior vehicle finished in highly polished natural wood and the pride of the fleet. The final addition was two cars purchased in 1928 from Dumbarton.

Ayr was a progressive tramway undertaking, which continually improved the infrastructure, relaying track and renovating cars as late as 1931. Unfortunately at the end of that year the Scottish Motor Traction Company offered to buy the undertaking. The offer was accepted and SMT buses took over on 1 January 1932 under an agreement valid for 21 years. The trams had served the town well, especially at holiday weekends, when crowds would be transported to the Burns Monument at one end of the line and to Prestwick at the other.

Glasgow Subway

Returning to Glasgow Central Station by electric train from Ayr, we can, by walking about 400 yards to St. Enoch Station, transfer to the Glasgow Subway. This 6½ mile circular 'tube' line of four-foot gauge connecting central Glasgow with Govan and the inner suburbs to the west and south, was opened by the Glasgow District Subway Company in 1897,and worked then by cable traction with fifty bogie cars. It was purchased by the Corporation in 1923 and electrified in 1935 on the third-rail principle, the inner circle in March and the outer in December. Some of the rolling stock was renovated using new steel underframes from Hurst Nelson and electrical equipment from Metropolitan Vickers.

The subway then operated successfully for over forty years until it was closed in 1977 for modernisation. The 'Clockwork Orange', as it was dubbed, re-opened on 16 April 1980 with refurbished stations and 33 new Metro-Cammell cars, which operate as two or three-car units with automatic train control.

Glasgow Garden Festival

The third garden festival in 1988 following those at Liverpool and Stoke-on-Trent was located on the site of the Princes Dock adjacent to Paisley Road Toll and the one-time tramway to Govan. It was the first to include a tramway and opened to the public on 28 April 1988. The first trams, Glasgow 22, Paisley 68 and Glasgow 1297, all from the National Tramway Museum at Crich, arrived at the site on 26 January, and on 13 February No. 22 became the first tram to run in Glasgow for exactly 25 years! Blackpool open boat car 606 arrived on 3 March, and Edinburgh 35, also from Blackpool, arrived on 11 March.

The tramway, 0.625 miles, approx. 1 Km., carried 1,560,641 passengers during the 152 days of the Festival which closed on 26 September, No. 68 being the last tram to enter the depot. The Glasgow and Edinburgh trams left for Crich on 9 October, Paisley 68 on 10 October, and Blackpool 606 left the depot for home on 25 October.

Glasgow Museum of Transport

This museum, initially located in the paint shop of former car works at Coplawhill, was re-opened on 21 April 1988 in the more spacious Kelvin Hall. The exhibits include former horse tramcar No. 543 of 1896, single-deck 'Room & Kitchen' No. 672 of 1898, 'Round-dash' standard No. 779 of 1900, 'Hex-dash' standard No. 1088 of 1924, experimental single-deck bogie car No. 1089 of 1926, Coronation No. 1173 of 1938, and Cunarder No. 1392 of 1952. In addition there is Subway trailer car T39 and a mock-up of a Subway station.

Other Preserved Glasgow Tramcars

Standard cars Nos. 22 and 812, No. 1055(ii) restored as Liverpool 869, ex-Paisley No. 1068, Kilmarnock bogies Nos. 1100 and 1115, Coronation No. 1282, Cunarder No. 1297, and two works cars, No. 1 plus trailer and No. 21, are at the National Tramway Museum, Crich, Derbyshire, England. Standard car No. 585 is at the Science Museum in London and No. 488 is at the AMTUIR Museum in Paris.

Coronation No. 1245 after time at the East Anglia Museum at Carlton Colville near Lowestoft is now, 2002, in store at Blackpool, and Coronation No. 1274 is at Kennebunckport, Maine, USA.

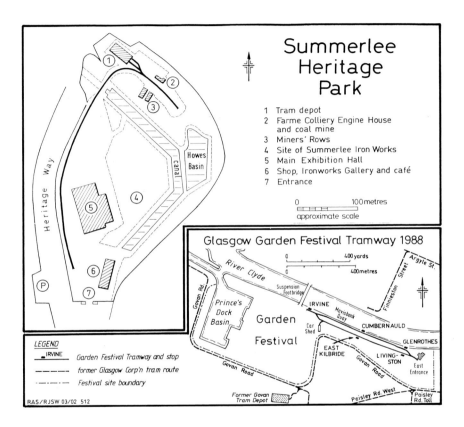

Summerlee Heritage Park

1 Tram depot
2 Farme Colliery Engine House and coal mine
3 Miners' Rows
4 Site of Summerlee Iron Works
5 Main Exhibition Hall
6 Shop, Ironworks Gallery and café
7 Entrance

0   100 metres
approximate scale

Glasgow Garden Festival Tramway 1988

LEGEND
━■IRVINE   Garden Festival Tramway and stop
----------   former Glasgow Corp'n tram route
—·—·—   Festival site boundary

RAS/RJSW 03/02 512

Summerlee Heritage Trust

Located in Coatbridge, adjacent to Coatbridge Central Station, and near Coatbridge Sunnyside, this open-air museum has been developed on the site of the Sunnyside Ironworks which closed in 1932. The Museum claims to be the noisiest museum in the country, and in addition to exhibiting life and work in the area there is a half-mile tramway, opened in 1988, running from the entrance along two sides of the site, which includes a branch of the Monkland Canal.

The initial rolling stock was Bruxelles 9062 and Graz 225, but the main attraction now is restored Lanarkshire Tramways Class M open-top car No. 53. The lower saloon of this car was rescued from a field near Irvine. In addition the lower saloons of two ex-Paisley cars, Glasgow numbers 1016 and 1017, are on the premises, and the latter is being restored to single-deck condition as the Glasgow School Car.

Locomotive No. 4, 'Sir Murray Morrison' with the LRTL party on the line of the British Aluminium Company Ltd. at Fort William. 5 August 1955. *(R. J. S. Wiseman*

Minor Lines

Nearest to Glasgow, but well to the west, and six miles due south of Greenock, was the moorland light railway on **Duchall Moor**. It was opened in 1911 and carried visitors in the grouse-shooting season by means of a petrol tractor on 60cm. track. There were nearly eight miles of track, consisting of four lines serving the higher hills at over 1,000 feet.

At **Kinlochleven** the British Aluminium Company Ltd. opened in 1908 a short electric freight line from its factory down to the pier on Loch Leven. There were three totally-enclosed locomotives, and the overhead equipment was of typical street tramway type with current collection by pantograph. The line closed in 1959. This Company also operated a lengthy 20-mile 3ft. gauge line out to and over the hills from its pier at **Fort William** to another pier at Loch Treig. The various lines were in use between 1925 and 1977, and used steam, petrol and diesel powered stock.

Far to the west on the **Kintyre** Peninsula was the 2ft. 3in. gauge Campbeltown and Machrihanish Light Railway, a purely steam passenger line opened in 1876 and closed in 1932. However the 1905 powers under which the line was purchased by the Argyle Railway Co., Ltd. from the Campbeltown Coal Co., Ltd. included permission to electrify it. This little 6¼ mile line was no less than 35 miles from the nearest other railway, at Ardrossan.

A steamer trip from Oban to **Craignure** on the Isle of Mull is well worth while. From Craignure Old Pier a short 1¼-mile 10¼ in. gauge steam tourist railway, opened in 1984, is operated during the season along the coast to Torosay Castle.

Finally, in the **Western Isles**, the Hebridean Light Railway Co., Ltd., whose title concealed an over-optimistic intention, had hoped in 1898 to build a 97-mile line on the 3ft. 6in. gauge in the counties of Inverness and Ross, partly on the Isle of Skye and partly on Harris and Lewis. It was hoped to get a free grant from the treasury, but when this was refused the scheme collapsed. Twenty years later Lord Leverhulme purchased Lewis and planned about 100 miles of 3ft. gauge overhead hydro-electric railway for Lewis and Harris. Construction was started near Stornoway in 1920 but the scheme was then dropped.

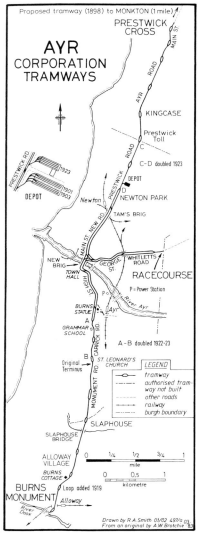

Above:- Ayr No. 9 at Rozells Wood en-route to the Burns Monument beyond Alloway
village. *(South Ayrshire Libraries, courtesy R. W. Brash*

Below:- One of the 1908 Dick Kerr Locomotives at the Kinlochleven Aluminium Works
of the British Aluminium Company Ltd. 5 August 1955. *(J. C. Gillham*

TRAMCAR VARIETY AT AYR

No. 22 in original open-top, front-exit, condition at the Racecourse terminus. Note the unusual upper-deck lamp. *(Courtesy National Tramway Museum*

No.28 dates from 1899 and was bought third hand from Manchester Corporation in 1922. At the Racecourse terminus. *(South Ayrshire Libraries*

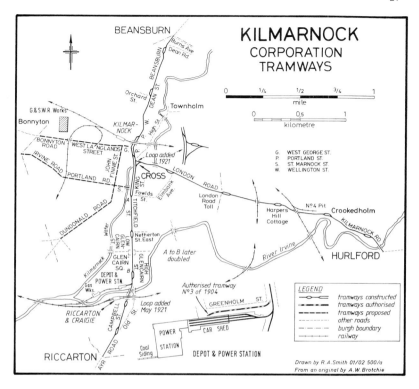

KILMARNOCK
CORPORATION
TRAMWAYS

BEANSBURN

Burns Ave
Dean Rd

Orchard St.
Townholm

G & S.W.R. Works
Bonnyton

KILMAR-NOCK

BONNYTON ROAD
WEST LANGLANDS STREET
IRVINE ROAD
PORTLAND RD.
JOHN FINNIE ST.

Loop added 1921

CROSS

LONDON ROAD

G.   WEST GEORGE ST.
P.   PORTLAND ST.
S.   ST. MARNOCK ST.
W.   WELLINGTON ST.

DUNDONALD ROAD

Fowlds St.
Elmbank Ave.

London Road Toll

Harpers Hill Cottage

Nº 4 Pit
Crookedholm

KILMARNOCK RD.

Water St.
GLEN CAIRN St.
Netherton St.East

GLENCAIRN SQ.

Kilmarnock
DEPOT & POWER STN.

Gas Wks.

A to B later doubled

River Irvine

HURLFORD

Authorised tramway Nº 3 of 1904

GREENHOLM ST.

Loop added May 1921

RICCARTON & CRAIGIE

CAMPBELL ST.
AYR ROAD

POWER STATION
CAR SHED
Coal Siding

RICCARTON

DEPOT & POWER STATION

LEGEND
tramways constructed
tramways authorised
tramways proposed
other roads
burgh boundary
railway

Drawn by R.A.Smith 01/02 500/a
From an original by A.W.Brotchie

Kilmarnock cars were all supplied by Hurst Nelson. Open-top No. 8 is seen at Crookedholm loop on the approach to Hurlford. *(N.B.Traction Collection*

TRAMCAR VARIETY

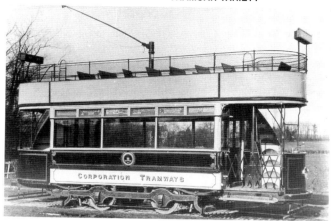

Kilmarnock No. 8
as delivered from
Hurst Nelson in
1904.

*(North
Lanarkshire
Council*

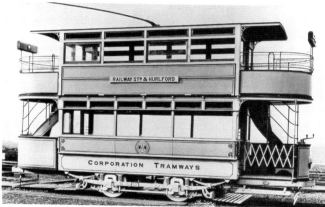

One of the two
top-covered
cars, Nos. 13, 14,
as delivered to
Kilmarnock from
Hurst Nelson in
1905.

*(North
Lanarkshire
Council*

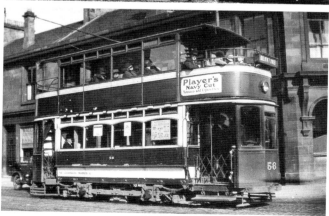

No. 56 was
similar to No. 88
but built in the
Company's
workshops.
Photographed at
Hamilton, New
Cross, on a
short working to
Blantyre.

*(Dr. H. A.
Whitcombe,
Science Museum,
Science and
Picture Library*

THE LANARKSHIRE TRAMWAYS

Ornate brackets were a feature of the company systems. UEC No. 48 is in Main Street, Wishaw, en-route to Motherwell.
(Commercial card, courtesy National Tramway Museum

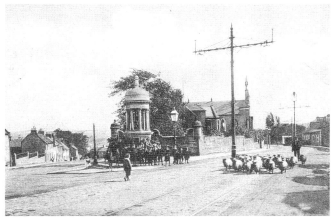

Sheep and the scrollwork on the poles make an interesting study at the Watson Fountain, Hamilton. There is an open-top tram in the distance.
(Commercial card, courtesy National Tramway Museum

No. 88 was built by Hurst Nelson in 1925. It is seen outside the Power House and depot, on Clyde Street, Motherwell, in 1929.
(Dr. H. A. Whitcombe, Science Museum, Science and Picture Library

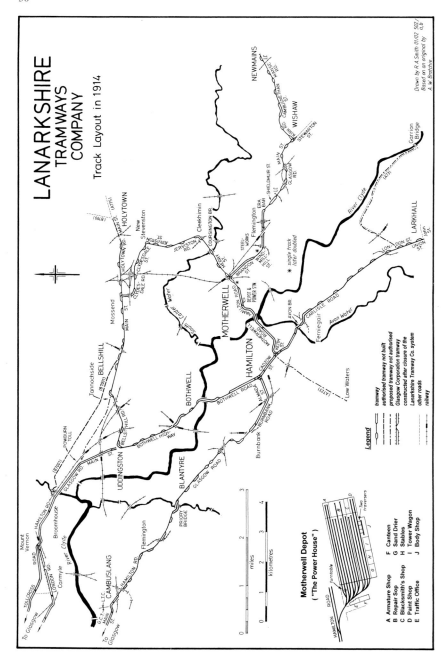

LANARKSHIRE TRAMWAYS COMPANY

Track Layout in 1914

Drawn by R A Smith 01/02 502 / a,b
Based on an original by A W Brotchie

Legend

tramway
authorised tramway not built
proposed tramway not authorised
Glasgow Corporation tramway
constructed after closure of the
Lanarkshire Tramway Co. system
other roads
railway

* single track later doubled

Motherwell Depot
("The Power House")

A Armature Shop
B Repair Sop
C Blacksmith's Shop
D Paint Shop
E Traffic Office
F Canteen
G Sand Drier
H Stables
I Tower Wagon
J Body Shop

NEWMAINS
WISHAW
LARKHALL
Garrion Bridge
HOLYTOWN
New Stevenston
Cleekhimin
Coursington Br
MOTHERWELL
HAMILTON
BELLSHILL
Mossend
Tannochside
BOTHWELL
UDDINGSTON
BLANTYRE
Burnbank
Low Waters
Flemington
Steel-works
Avon Br
Ferniegair
Mount Vernon
Broomhouse
CAMBUSLANG
Priory Bridge
Flemington
To Glasgow
Tollcross

miles
kilometres

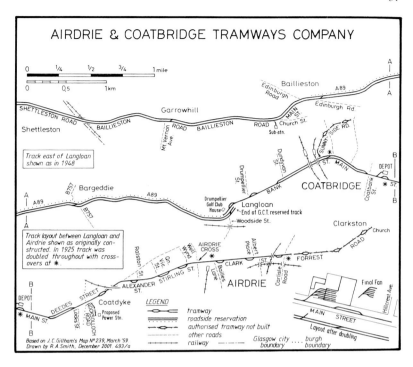

On 8 August 1953 Coronation 1244 passes St. Johns Church in Coatbridge on its long haul to Gairbraid Avenue some miles beyond St. Georges Cross. Did the local burghers know where Gairbraid Avenue was?
(R. J. S. Wiseman

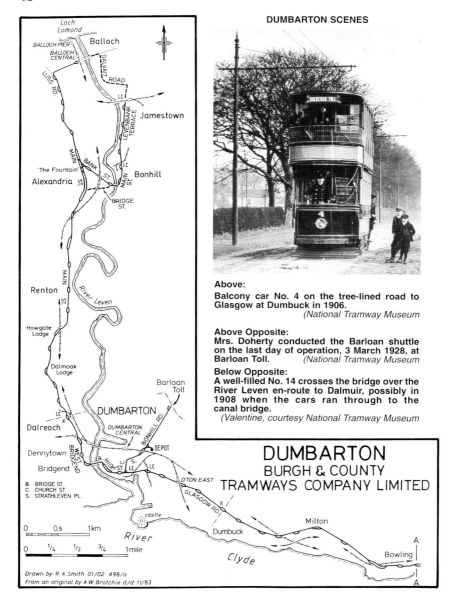

DUMBARTON SCENES

Above:
Balcony car No. 4 on the tree-lined road to Glasgow at Dumbuck in 1906.
(National Tramway Museum

Above Opposite:
Mrs. Doherty conducted the Barloan shuttle on the last day of operation, 3 March 1928, at Barloan Toll. *(National Tramway Museum*

Below Opposite:
A well-filled No. 14 crosses the bridge over the River Leven en-route to Dalmuir, possibly in 1908 when the cars ran through to the canal bridge.
(Valentine, courtesy National Tramway Museum

DUMBARTON
BURGH & COUNTY
TRAMWAYS COMPANY LIMITED

Loch Lomond

BALLOCH PIER Balloch

BALLOCH CENTRAL

DALVAIT ROAD

LUSS RD.

LC

Jamestown

LEVENBANK TERRACE

MAIN ST. BANK ST.

'The Fountain'

Alexandria

LC Bonhill

BRIDGE ST.

Renton

River Leven

MAIN ST.

Howgate Lodge

Dalmoak Lodge

Barloan Toll

DUMBARTON

Dalreoch

DUMBARTON CENTRAL

BONHILL RD.

Dennytown

Bridgend

WEST BRIDGEND

HIGH ST.

B. C. S.

LC

LC

DEPOT

D'TON EAST

GLASGOW RD.

B. BRIDGE ST.
C. CHURCH ST.
S. STRATHLEVEN PL.

castle

0   0.5   1km

0   1/4   1/2   3/4   1mile

River

Dumbuck

Clyde

Milton

Bowling

A

A

Drawn by R.A.Smith 01/02 498/a
From an original by A.W.Brotchie d/d 11/83

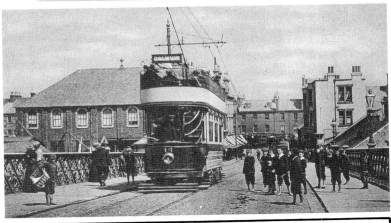

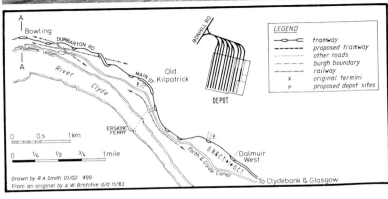

34

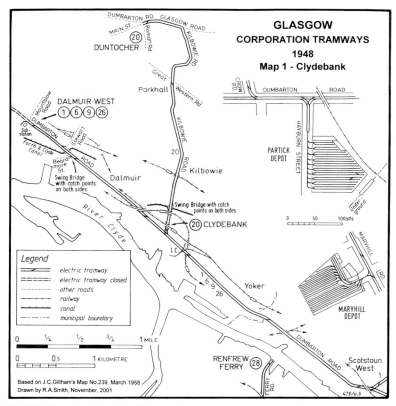

No. 1012 was converted to single-deck for the Duntocher service in 1925. At Duntocher terminus in 1939. *(W. A. Camwell, National Tramway Museum*

SERVING GLASGOW SHIPYARDS

'Baillie Burts's Car' or 'Wee Baldie' No. 1089 of 1926, which from 1952 worked shipyard specials from John Brown's at Clydebank. Seen at Scotstoun on 10 August 1954.

(R. J. S. Wiseman

Kilmarnock bogie No. 1102 at Scotstoun awaits departure for Rutherglen, while No. 1127 has just arrived. 4 August 1955.

(R. J. S. Wiseman

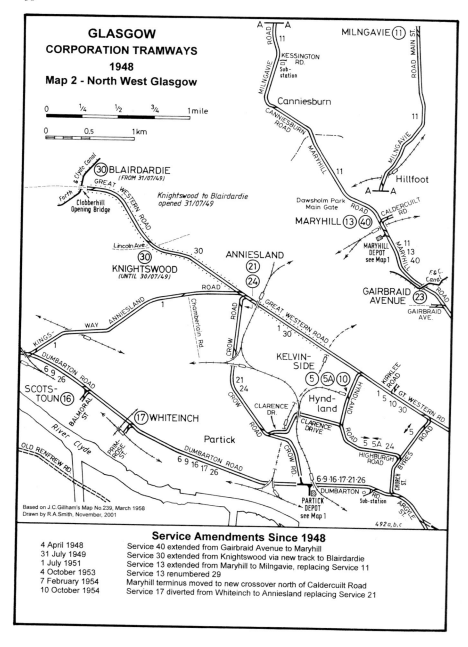

GLASGOW
CORPORATION TRAMWAYS
1948
Map 2 - North West Glasgow

0   ¼   ½   ¾   1mile

0   0.5   1km

BLAIRDARDIE (30) (FROM 31/07/49)

Forth & Clyde Canal

Clobberhill Opening Bridge

Knightswood to Blairdardie opened 31/07/49

GREAT WESTERN ROAD

Lincoln Ave.

KNIGHTSWOOD (30) (UNTIL 30/07/49)

ANNIESLAND (21) (24)

ROAD

Chamberlain Rd.

CROW ROAD

ANNIESLAND

WAY

KINGS-

DUMBARTON ROAD

6 9 26

SCOTS-TOUN (16)

BALMORAL ST.

(17) WHITEINCH

PRIMROSE ST.

River Clyde

OLD RENFREW RD.

Partick

DUMBARTON ROAD
6 9 16 17 26

GREAT WESTERN ROAD
1 30

KELVIN-SIDE

(5) (5A) (10)

CROW ROAD

CLARENCE DR.

Hynd-land

CLARENCE DRIVE

CROW RD.

6·9·16·17·21·26
DUMBARTON
PARTICK DEPOT see Map 1

Sub-station

MILNGAVIE ROAD

KESSINGTON RD.
Sub-station

MILNGAVIE ROAD

11

A   A
11

Canniesburn

CANNIESBURN ROAD

MARYHILL

11

MILNGAVIE (11)

ROAD MAIN ST.

MILNGAVIE ROAD

11

Hillfoot

A   A

Dawsholm Park Main Gate

ROAD

CALDERCUILT RD.

MARYHILL (13) (40)

MARYHILL DEPOT see Map1

MARYHILL

11
13
40

F.&C. Canal

GAIRBRAID AVENUE (23)

GAIRBRAID AVE.

KIRKLEE ROAD

1 5 10 30

GT. WESTERN RD.

HYNDLAND ROAD

5 5A 24

HIGHBURGH ROAD

CHURCH ST.

BYRES RD.

ARGYLE ST.

5

492 a,b,c

Based on J.C.Gillham's Map No.239, March 1958
Drawn by R.A.Smith, November, 2001

Service Amendments Since 1948

4 April 1948	Service 40 extended from Gairbraid Avenue to Maryhill
31 July 1949	Service 30 extended from Knightswood via new track to Blairdardie
1 July 1951	Service 13 extended from Maryhill to Milngavie, replacing Service 11
4 October 1953	Service 13 renumbered 29
7 February 1954	Maryhill terminus moved to new crossover north of Caldercuilt Road
10 October 1954	Service 17 diverted from Whiteinch to Anniesland replacing Service 21

Great Western Road, Glasgow.

Glasgow No. 541 in original open-top condition passes the Byers Road junction as it heads up the Great Western Road towards Anniesland.
(Courtesy National Tramway Museum

No. 961, newly fitted with top cover, is posed on the Great Western Road, alongside the Botanic Gardens.
(Courtesy National Tramway Museum

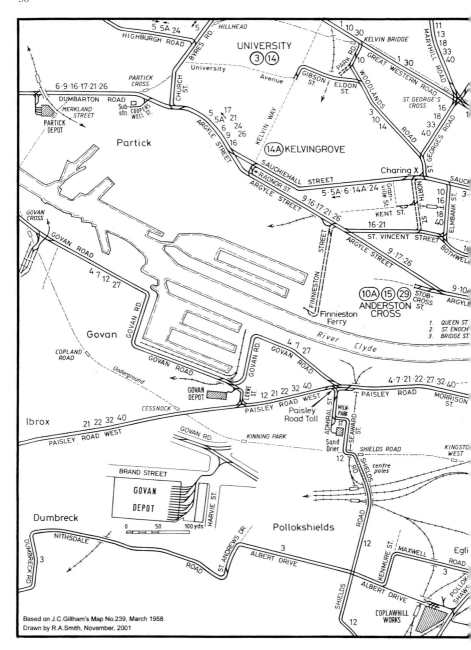

Based on J.C.Gillham's Map No.239, March 1958
Drawn by R.A.Smith, November, 2001

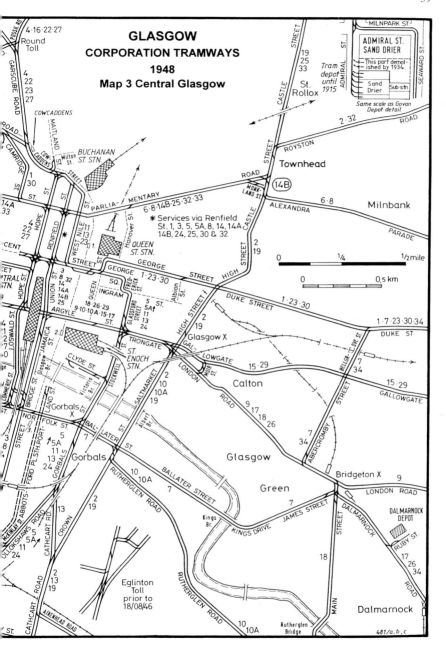

GLASGOW
CORPORATION TRAMWAYS
1948
Map 3 Central Glasgow

ADMIRAL ST.
SAND DRIER

This part demol-
ished by 1934.

Sand
Drier | Sub-stn

Same scale as Govan
Depot detail

Tram
depot
until
1915

St.
Rollox

2·32

COWCADDENS

BUCHANAN
ST. STN.

Townhead

14B

Milnbank

ALEXANDRA

6·8

PARADE

* Services via Renfield
St. 1, 3, 5, 5A, 8, 14, 14A,
14B, 24, 25, 30 & 32

QUEEN
ST. STN.

6·8·14B·25·32·33

GEORGE
SQ.

INGRAM

George Street

HIGH

1·23·30

DUKE STREET

1·23·30

1·7·23·30·34

DUKE ST.

Glasgow X

TRONGATE

ST.
ENOCH
STN.

CLYDE ST.

LOWGATE

15·29

Calton

15·29

GALLOWGATE

9
17
18
26

7
34

Gorbals
X

Glasgow

Gorbals

Bridgeton X 9

Green

LONDON ROAD

DALMARNOCK
DEPOT

Kings
Br.

KINGS DRIVE

JAMES STREET

18

Eglinton
Toll
prior to
18/08/46

Dalmarnock

10
10A

Rutherglen
Bridge

481/a,b,c

0   1/4   1/2 mile

0   0.5 km

GREAT WESTERN ROAD – 2

Standard No. 874 takes the second curve into Anniesland Road on 11 September 1954.
(R. J. S. Wiseman

Standard No. 208 on service 21 from Elderslie, is at Crow Road terminus, Anniesland, on 11 September 1954, approximately one month before this service was curtailed to St. Vincent Street. Service 17 was then diverted to Anniesland in its place. The tram in the background is on the Great Western Road heading west.
(R. J. S. Wiseman

Standard No. 231 leaves the Blairdardie terminus on 4 September 1954 for Dalmarnock. The plans to extend the trams further west were frustrated to some extent by another canal bridge.
(R. J. S. Wiseman

CITY CENTRE CONTRASTS

On 3 April 1953 the streets were still relatively free of motor traffic, as the lady waits for No. 1159, which, held up by the horse-drawn dray, waits to turn into West Nile Street. Trolleybuses took over as far as Queens Cross two months later.   *(R. J. S. Wiseman*

In October 1953 Service 29 was diverted from Anderston Cross to Milngavie in place of the 13. Ex-Liverpool cars were introduced in 1953 on this service, and No. 1024 is seen in St. Vincent Street on 7 August 1954.
                                                                                 (R. J. S. Wiseman

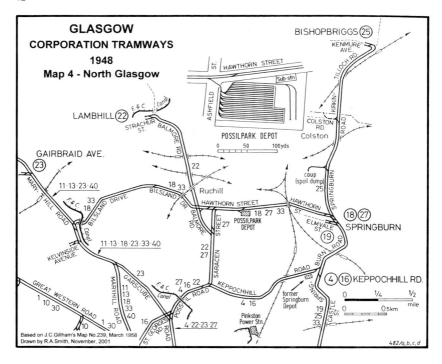

GLASGOW
CORPORATION TRAMWAYS
1948
Map 4 - North Glasgow

BISHOPBRIGGS 25

KENMURE AVE

HAWTHORN STREET

Sub-stn

LAMBHILL 22

ASHFIELD

STRACHUR ST.

BALMORE RD

F.&C. Canal

COLSTON RD.

Colston

POSSILPARK DEPOT

0   50   100yds

GAIRBRAID AVE.

23

22

MARYHILL ROAD

F.&C. Canal

11·13·23·40

33
18

BILSLAND DRIVE

18 33

Ruchill

HAWTHORN STREET

coup
(spoil dump)
25

SPRINGBURN

KELVINSIDE AVENUE

11·13·18·23·33·40

BALMORE RD.

SARACEN STREET

27

18 27 33
POSSILPARK
DEPOT

HAWTHORN ST.

ELMVALE ST.

18 27

19

SPRINGBURN

22
27

22
27

BURN ROAD

GREAT WESTERN ROAD

GARSCUBE ROAD

23

MARYHILL ROAD

F.&C. Canal

27 16 22
4

POSSIL ROAD

KEPPOCHHILL

4 16

ROAD

SPRING

CASTLE ST.

4 16 KEPPOCHHILL RD.

1 10 30

11
13
18
33
40

10

1 30

16

ST. GEORGES ROAD

4·22·23·27

former
Springburn
Depot

Pinkston
Power Stn.

0   1/4   1/2
mile
0   0.5km

19
25
33

Based on J.C.Gillham's Map No.239, March 1958
Drawn by R.A.Smith, November, 2001

482/a,b,c,d

Lambhill was served by service 22 from Crookston and 31 from Pollokshaws on 7 August 1953. Did the driver of No. 1372 have time to visit the café before departure back to Govan depot?   *(R. J. S. Wiseman)*

THE NORTHERN SUBURBS

In north Glasgow the trams went under the canal. In this view No. 374 is about to pass under the Possil Road aqueduct on its way to Springburn. *(R. J. S. Wiseman*

They also went under railways. Here No. 994, working from Springburn to Linthouse, is taking the dip down under the main line from Queen Street to Edinburgh on 27 July 1954. *(R. J. S. Wiseman*

44

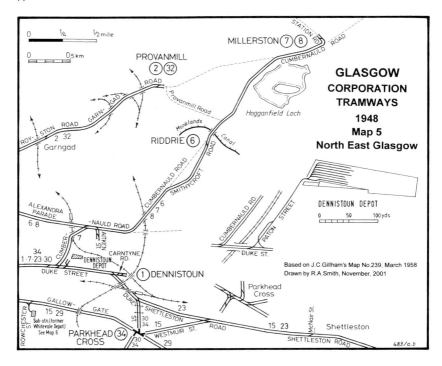

0   ¼   ½ mile

0   0.5 km

PROVANMILL
(2)(32)

MILLERSTON (7)(8)

ROAD

GARN-GAD

ROYSTON ROAD

2 32
Garngad

Provanmill Road

CUMBERNAULD ROAD

Hogganfield Loch

RIDDRIE (6)

Monklands
Canal

**GLASGOW
CORPORATION
TRAMWAYS
1948
Map 5
North East Glasgow**

CUMBERNAULD ROAD

SMITHYCROFT ROAD

2 7 6

8

ALEXANDRA
PARADE
6 8

-NAULD ROAD

7

AITKEN ST.

CARNTYNE
RD.

34
1·7·23·30

CUMBER-

DENNISTOUN
DEPOT

CUMBERNAULD RD.

PATON STREET

DUKE ST.

DENNISTOUN DEPOT

0   50   100 yds

DUKE   STREET

(1) DENNISTOUN

Parkhead
Cross

Based on J.C.Gillham's Map No.239, March 1958
Drawn by R.A.Smith, November, 2001

GALLOW-   GATE

15 29

ROWCHESTER ST.

Sub-stn.(former
Whitevale Depot)
See Map 5

PARKHEAD
CROSS

DUKE ST.

SHETTLESTON

30
34   15

23

WESTMUIR ST.

ROAD

30
34   29

15 23

McNair St.

Shettleston

SHETTLESTON ROAD

(34)

483/a.b

Liverpool car 1011 leaving Parkhead depot on 8 April 1958.   *(R. J. S. Wiseman*

BUSY SCENES ON THE ROAD TO MILLERSTON

A busy scene at Riddrie terminus on 10 August 1955. No. 1236 is bound for Rouken Glen, while the four cars behind will either reverse or continue on to Millerston.
(R. J. S. Wiseman

Further out No. 655 from Govan is disgorging passengers at Hogganfield Loch, a popular destination on sunny days. 17 April 1955. *(R. J. S. Wiseman*

46

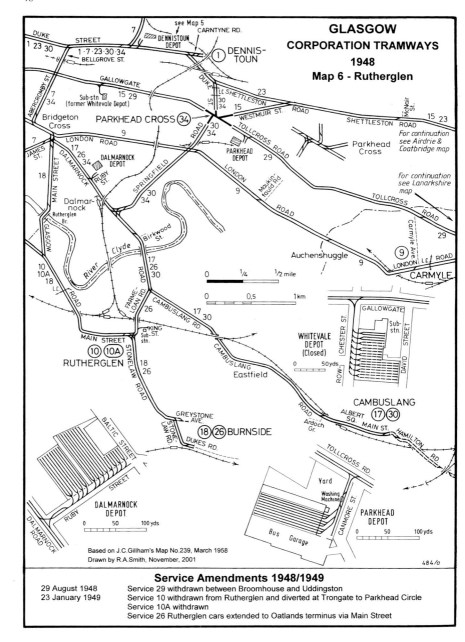

Service Amendments 1948/1949

29 August 1948	Service 29 withdrawn between Broomhouse and Uddingston
23 January 1949	Service 10 withdrawn from Rutherglen and diverted at Trongate to Parkhead Circle
	Service 10A withdrawn
	Service 26 Rutherglen cars extended to Oatlands terminus via Main Street

RUTHERGLEN JUNCTIONS

The Burgh of Rutherglen was served by services 10, 18 and 26 until the 10 was withdrawn in January 1949 and the Rutherglen part of the 26 extended in its place as far as Oatlands. This view from Stonelaw Road sees No. 569 turning left into Main Street on 10 August 1953.

(R. J. S. Wiseman

Nearly two years later on 14 April 1955 No. 323 was also viewed from the Stonelaw Road. It has just turned into Farmeloan Road on service 26 to Scotstoun via Dalmarnock and Partick.

(R. J. S. Wiseman

48

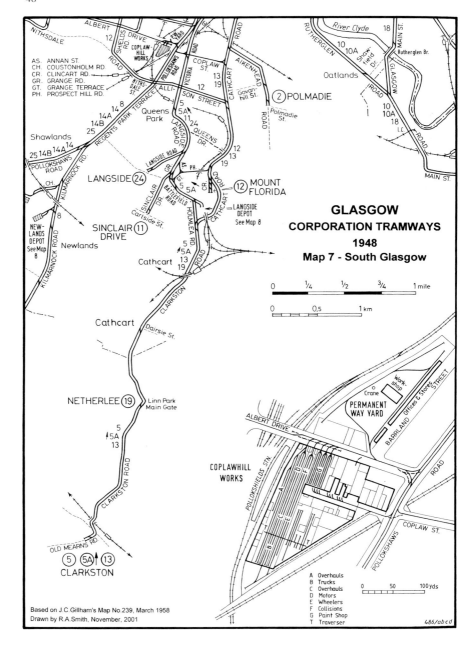

AS. ANNAN ST.
CH. COUSTONHOLM RD.
CR. CLINCART RD.
GR. GRANGE RD.
GT. GRANGE TERRACE
PH. PROSPECT HILL RD.

POLMADIE

Oatlands

Shawlands

Queens Park

LANGSIDE (24)

MOUNT FLORIDA

NEW-LANDS DEPOT
See Map 8

SINCLAIR (11) DRIVE

Newlands

LANGSIDE DEPOT
See Map 8

GLASGOW
CORPORATION TRAMWAYS
1948
Map 7 - South Glasgow

0   ¼   ½   ¾   1 mile

0   0,5   1 km

Cathcart

Cathcart

Dairsie St.

NETHERLEE (19)   Linn Park Main Gate

PERMANENT WAY YARD

Work Shop

Crane

COPLAWHILL WORKS

COPLAW ST.

OLD MEARNS RD.

(5) (5A) (13)
CLARKSTON

0   50   100 yds

A Overhauls
B Trucks
C Overhauls
D Motors
E Wheelers
F Collisions
G Paint Shop
T Traverser

Based on J.C.Gillham's Map No.239, March 1958
Drawn by R.A.Smith, November, 2001

486/abcd

LANGSIDE SCENES

After the conversion of the Clarkston route to trolleybuses on 5 July 1953 the 5 service terminated at Holmlea Road. Standard No. 341 and Coronation 1152 form a contrast at the new terminus on 3 April 1955. *(R. J. S. Wiseman*

The Cathcart area routes were served by Langside depot, as were services 2 to Polmadie and 19 to Netherlee. Standard No. 9 with appropriate destination screens was photographed in Langside depot on 11 August 1953. *(R. J. S. Wiseman*

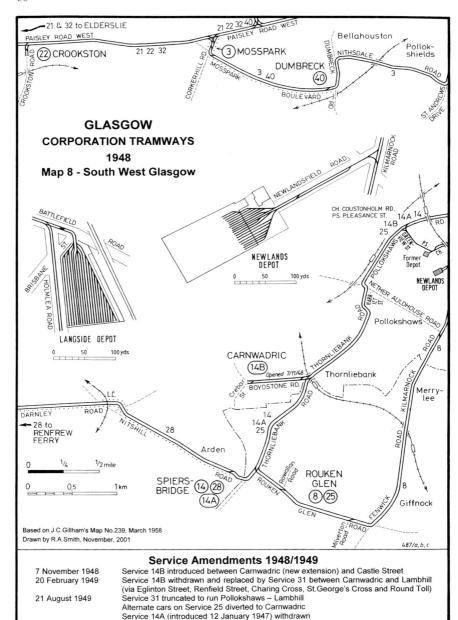

GLASGOW
CORPORATION TRAMWAYS
1948
Map 8 - South West Glasgow

Based on J.C.Gillham's Map No.239, March 1958
Drawn by R.A.Smith, November, 2001

487/a,b,c

Service Amendments 1948/1949

7 November 1948	Service 14B introduced between Carnwadric (new extension) and Castle Street
20 February 1949	Service 14B withdrawn and replaced by Service 31 between Carnwadric and Lambhill (via Eglinton Street, Renfield Street, Charing Cross, St.George's Cross and Round Toll)
21 August 1949	Service 31 truncated to run Pollokshaws – Lambhill
	Alternate cars on Service 25 diverted to Carnwadric
	Service 14A (introduced 12 January 1947) withdrawn

POLLOKSHIELDS

Cunarder 1328 from Mosspark is about to leave the fare station at Shields Road crossing. Here it crossed service 12, Linthouse-Mount Florida. 9 August 1953.
(R. J. S. Wiseman

Standard No. 90 is almost alone on tree-lined Nithsdale Road at Erskine Avenue. 30 July 1955.
(R. J. S. Wiseman

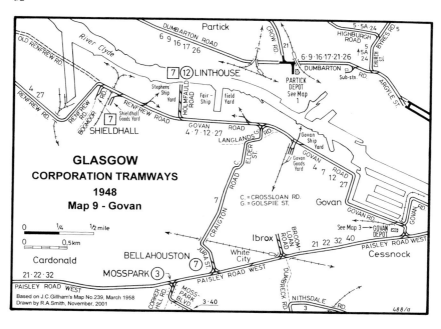

The blue Fairfield locomotive (English Electric No. 1131 of 1940) in action along the Govan Road, at Golspie Street junctions, on its 500 yard journey from the shipyard to the Govan Goods depot.

(M. G. C. W. Wheeler

SERVING GOVAN SHIPYARDS

The four right-angle bends on Govan Road were necessary to avoid the three Princes Docks. Standard No. 266 on Service 7, 'The Yellow Peril', is turning the corner on to the West Quay by the main entrance to all three Princes Docks. The ship is in the Graving Dock. These docks were the site of the Glasgow Garden Festival in 1988. 6 April 1958.
(R. J. S. Wiseman

Further to the west the Govan Shipbuilding Yard of Harland & Wolffe Ltd. dominated the north side of the road. No. 378 is about to accelerate away from the compulsory tram stop. 7 August 1954. The Subway passes beneath the tramway, where the bus is, close to Govan Cross.
(R. J. S. Wiseman

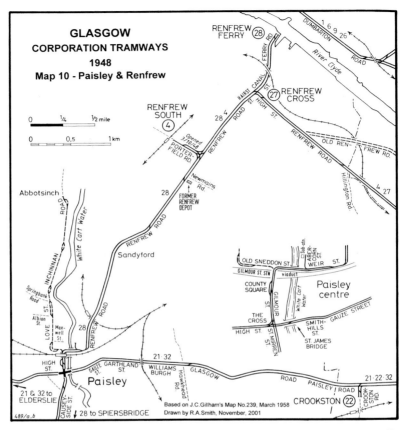

GLASGOW
CORPORATION TRAMWAYS
1948
Map 10 - Paisley & Renfrew

It was a straight, fast, run to Renfrew after the new road diverting round the new King George V Dock opened in 1926. Standard 403, destined for Renfrew South is at speed on 6 August 1953.
(R. J. S. Wiseman

BUSY JUNCTIONS AT GOVAN AND RENFREW

At Golspie Street junction, where service 7 trams turned left on the curve at the very bottom of the picture to Bellahouston, those on the 4,12 and 27 went straight ahead. No. 567, however, is an evening special from the shipyards to the University. Photographed on 7 August 1954 this car was withdrawn at the end of the year.
(R. J. S. Wiseman

At Renfrew South a new siding was laid in Porterfield Road in 1948 to serve the Babcock & Wilcox Works, and numerous specials were to be seen each evening. The 'Polis' has no problems as No. 909 moves on towards Paisley. 27 July 1955.
(R. J. S. Wiseman

TRAMS FROM GLASGOW TO BEYOND PAISLEY

An intensive service of buses and trams linked Glasgow with Paisley. Coronation 1273 leaves the fare stage at Halfway on 30 July 1955. *(R. J. S.Wiseman*

Paisley District No. 38 arrives at Johnstone Centre, probably sometime between 12 July 1904 and 4 July 1906, when the extension to Kilbarchan was opened. *(Commercial card, courtesy National Tramway Museum*

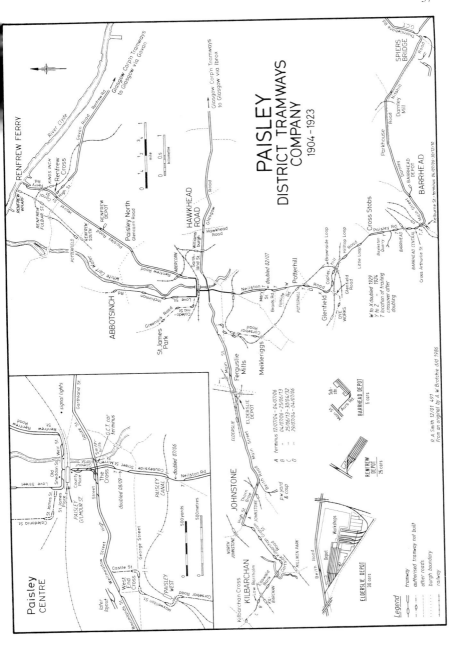

PAISLEY
DISTRICT TRAMWAYS
COMPANY
1904 - 1923

GLASGOW TRAMS IN RENFREW AND PAISLEY

Paisley local services formerly extended from Renfrew Ferry to Barrhead, but from 3 April 1949 to Glenfield only. No. 929, at the Ferry, awaits departure to Lochfield Road on 22 July 1954. The distant buildings are on the far side of the River Clyde.

(R. J. S. Wiseman

The Renfrew Ferry-Glenfield service in Paisley was known as 'The Goldmine'. Glasgow No. 103 loads up in Gilmour Street, Paisley on 6 April 1955.
(R. J. S. Wiseman

No. 301 on the 27 service to Springburn awaits departure from Renfrew. Cross on 27 July 1955.
(R. J. S. Wiseman

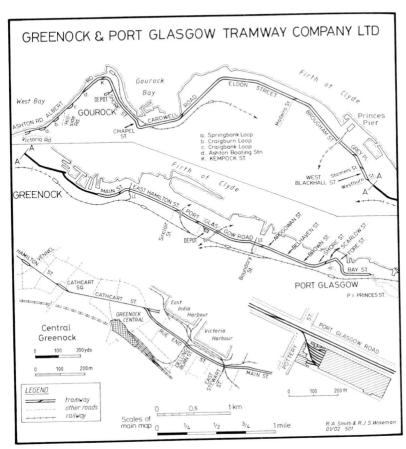

GREENOCK & PORT GLASGOW TRAMWAY COMPANY LTD

a. Springbank Loop
b. Craigburn Loop
c. Craigbank Loop
d. Ashton Boating Stn
K. KEMPOCK ST.

West Bay

Gourock Bay

Firth of Clyde

GOUROCK

Princes Pier

GREENOCK

Firth of Clyde

PORT GLASGOW

P = PRINCES ST.

Central Greenock

LEGEND

tramway
other roads
railway

Scales of main map

R.A.Smith & R.J.S.Wiseman
01/02 501

The Gourock end of the Greenock line. Balcony car No. 41 of 1911 stands alongside the Yacht Club House. *(Schwerdt-foger card, courtesy National Tramway Museum*

TRAMCARS AT GOUROCK

Cardwell Road, Gourock. Note fare stage No. 22, part of the BET 'Fair Fares system' with farthing stages.
(Reliable series, courtesy National Tramway Museum

The Greenock Company opened with thirty large bogie cars from Brush in 1901. The elaborate paintwork and the BET 'Magnet & Wheel' are clearly seen in this view.
(Commercial card, courtesy National Tramway Museum

No.10 was one of 30 large double-deck Brush cars delivered to the Greenock & Port Glasgow Tramway for the opening with electric traction on 3 October 1901. Believed photographed at the Gourock terminus.

(Dr. H. A. Whitcombe, Science Museum, Science and Society Picture Library

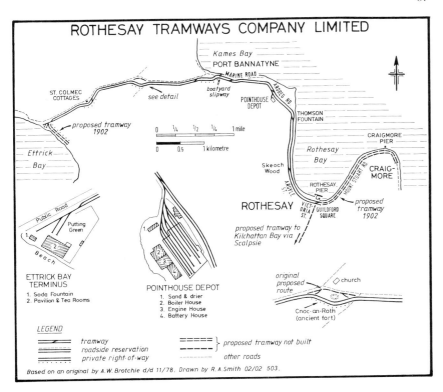

ROTHESAY TRAMWAYS COMPANY LIMITED

Kames Bay
PORT BANNATYNE
MARINE ROAD

ST. COLMEC
COTTAGES

see detail

boatyard
slipway

POINTHOUSE
DEPOT

THOMSON
FOUNTAIN

proposed tramway
1902

CRAIGMORE
PIER

Ettrick
Bay

Rothesay
Bay

Skeach
Wood

CRAIG-
MORE

ROTHESAY.
PIER

ROTHESAY

VICT-
ORIA
ST.

GUILDFORD
SQUARE

proposed
tramway
1902

proposed tramway to
Kilchattan Bay via
Scalpsie

Public Road

Putting
Green

1
2

Beach

0   1/4   1/2   1/4   1 mile

0   0.5   1 kilometre

**ETTRICK BAY
TERMINUS**
1. Soda Fountain
2. Pavilion & Tea Rooms

POINTHOUSE DEPOT
1. Sand & drier
2. Boiler House
3. Engine House
4. Battery House

original
proposed
route

church

Cnoc-an-Roth
(ancient fort)

LEGEND

tramway
roadside reservation
private right-of-way

proposed tramway not built
other roads

Based on an original by A.W. Brotchie d/d 11/78. Drawn by R.A.Smith 02/02 503.

A tram horse at the canter with one of the closed cars, Nos. 9-12, built by the Saville Street Foundry in Sheffield. *(Courtesy National Tramway Museum*

TRAMCAR VARIETY AT ROTHESAY

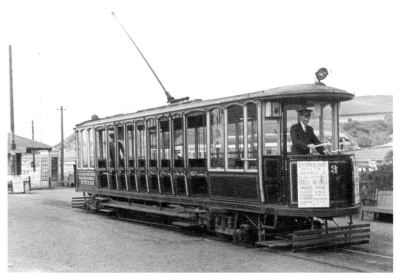

Crossbench car No. 3 at the Ettrick Bay terminus. *(C. Carter*

One of cars with open end compartments, No. 14, is seen at the Rothesay terminus.
(D. L. G.Hunter, courtesy A. W. Brotchie

THE GLASGOW — AIRDRIE INTERURBAN

The fine reserved tracks between Langloan and Ballieston linked the Airdrie and Glasgow systems in 1923, and Glasgow Coronation 1193 is seen heading for Airdrie on 4 April 1955.
(R. J. S. Wiseman

A very wet day in Airdrie as Coronation 1182 on service 15 loads passengers for Coatbridge or Glasgow, as a Baxter's bus loads, possibly for Clarkston, the authorised tram terminus. 18 August 1956.
(R. J. S. Wiseman

Tramcar Fleet Lists

All cars were double-deck unless otherwise stated.

Seating figures shown 22/34 for lower and upper decks respectively.

The opening date shown is the first day of regular public service.

The closing date for horse and steam operated tramways is the day the service closed, in many cases under a different operator. For electric services it is the last day of full public service.

Airdrie and Coatbridge Tramways Company

3.63 miles, 4ft. 7¾in. gauge. Opened 8 February 1904. Operated by the Airdrie and Coatbridge Tramway Trust from 30 September 1920 until 31 December 1921. Then linked to the Glasgow Corporation system. Closed 3 September 1966. Livery maroon and cream.

Car numbers	Type (as built)	Year built	Builder	Seats	Truck(s)	Motors	Controllers
1-12 (a)	Open top	1904	Brush	22/34	Brush AA	Brush 1002 2 x 25hp	Brush H2
13-15 (b)	Balcony	1905	Brush	22/34	Brush Conaty Radial	Brush 1002 2 x 25hp	Brush HD2

Notes

(a) Renumbered 1073-1084 in the Glasgow fleet.
(b) Nos.13 and 15 originally open top. Renumbered 1085-1087 in the Glasgow fleet.

Ardrossan, Saltcoats and District Tramways Company

6.26 miles authorised in 1906, 5.30 miles not authorised. 4ft. 8½in. gauge. The scheme was finally abandoned in 1914.

Ayr Corporation Tramways

6.36 miles, 4ft.8½in. gauge. Opened 26 September 1901, closed 31 December 1931. Livery chocolate and cream.

Car numbers	Type (as built)	Year built	Builder	Seats	Truck(s)	Motors	Controllers
1-10 (a)	Open top	1901	Hurst Nelson	22/35	HN Cantilever	BTH GE52-6T 2 x 20hp	BTH B18
11-16 (a)	Open top	1902	Hurst Nelson	22/37	HN Cantilever	BTH GE52 2 x 20hp	BTH BI8
17	Water car	1903	Hurst Nelson	—	Brill 21E	BTH GE52-6T 2 x 20hp	BTH B18
18 (b)	Open top	1902	Hurst Nelson	22/37	HN Cantilever	BTH GE52-6T 2 x 20hp	BTH B18
19-20 (c)	Open top	1907	Hurst Nelson	22/37	HN Solid forged	BTH GE52-6T 2 x 20hp	BTH B18
21-22 (d)	Open top	1913	Hurst Nelson	22/39	HN Solid forged	BTH GE52 2 x 20hp	BTH B18
23-24 (e)	Balcony	1915	Hurst Nelson	22/40	HN Solid forged	BTH GE58-6T 2 x 25hp	BTH B18
25-28 (f)	Single-deck	Bought 1922	Brush	26	Peckham Cantilever	BTH GE52-4T 2 x 25hp	BTH B18
29-30 (g)	Balcony	Bought 1928	EE	30/42	Peckham P22	GE 200K 2 x 40hp	BTH B18

Notes

(a) Nos.11-12 fitted HN 21E trucks ex-Kilmarnock in 1928; No.14 with truck ex-Kilmarnock or ex-Ayr 19. Nos. 1-10 reversed, 11-16 normal, stairs.
(b) Hurst Nelson Exhibition Car in London 1902. Purchased 1904.
(c) HN top covers fitted 1925, seating 22/36. No.19 fitted 60hp EE DK 105 motors, 1931, and Brill 79 E2 truck. No. 20 50hp BTH 509-M1 motors and BTH B510 controllers in 1930.
(d) Front exit cars. HN top covers fitted 1920, seating 22/40. Re-equipped as No.19 in 1931.
(e) Front exit cars. Re-equipped as No.19.
(f) Ex-Oldham, Ashton and Hyde Electric Tramways of series 1 - 26. Built in 1899 and purchased from Manchester Corporation in 1922. Believed new K10 controllers fitted.
(g) Ex-Dumbarton Nos. 31-32 regauged. Built 1921. Sold to South Shields Corporation in 1932, their Nos. 54, 57, later 16, 34.

Carstairs House Tramway

1.06 miles, 2ft. 6in. gauge. Opened in 1889, electric traction ceased c1895, horse traction c1924. Livery probably varnished teak.

Rolling stock consisted of one single-deck, single-truck car built at Carstairs seating 6 passengers and fitted with an 8hp motor. Also a number of goods vehicles.

Dumbarton Burgh and County Tramways

13.10 miles, 4ft. 7¾in. gauge. Opened 20 February 1907, closed 3 March 1928. Livery chocolate and cream, later green and cream.

Car Numbers	Type (as built)	Year Built	Builder	Seats	Truck(s)	Motors	Controllers
1-6 (a)	Balcony	1907	Brush	22/34	M&G 21EM	Westinghouse 200 2 x 30hp	Westinghouse 90M
7-26 (b)	Open top	1908	UEC	22/33	M&G 21EM	GE 54-3T 2 x 30hp	GE K2
27-30 (c)	Open top	Bought 1909	Various	18/32	Brill 21E	Westinghouse 49B 2 x 30hp	GE K10D
31-32 (d)	Balcony	1921	EE	30/42	Peckham P22	GE 200K 2 x 40hp	BTH B18

Notes

(a) Initial fleet was built for the Electric Supply Corporation which owned the system up to 31 December 1907. Later fitted with GE K10 controllers.
(b) Nos. 7, 8, 21 fitted with top covers ex-Falkirk in 1913.
(c) Ex-Glasgow Corporation horse trams, Nos. 24, 32, 47, 116, rebuilt for electric traction 1900-1. When used as single-deck cars on the Jamestown route the stairs to the upper-deck were blocked off.
(d) Sold to Ayr Corporation in 1928, Nos. 29-30. Sold in 1932 to South Shields.

Glasgow Tramway & Omnibus Company Ltd.

31.44 miles, 4ft. 7¾ ins. Horse traction. Opened 19 August 1872. The Company operated the lines in Glasgow until 30 June 1894 and those in Govan until 11 November 1896. Livery Menzies Tartan and white, later colour according to route, including blue, brown, chocolate, green, red, white and yellow.

The double-deck, open top uncanopied tramcars were numbered between 201 and 440 with a maximum of 233 at any one time. 114 cars were built by Tramway Car and Works Company of Greenwich, 54 by Stephenson of New York and 54 by the Metropolitan Railway Carriage and Wagon Company. There were also two single-deck open cars from Stephenson and similar cars were built in the Company's Crown Point Works. The Works also built numerous replacement double-deck cars over the years. 12 cars sold to Edinburgh and District Tramways Company.

Glasgow & Ibrox Tramways Company

1.55 miles, 4ft. 7¾in. Horse traction. Opened 18 July 1879. Purchased by the Govan Commissioners and operated by the G.T.& O from 28 May 1891. Livery possibly blue and cream.

Three open top Eades reversible cars by Ashbury, built 1878-79, and one single-deck car built in 1884.

Glasgow Corporation Tramways

31.44 miles, 4ft. 7¾in. gauge. Horse traction. Inaugurated 1 July 1894, last trams withdrawn on 14 April 1902. Livery crimson lake and cream plus route colour.

The fleet consisted of 364 new cars plus 21 ex-G.T.& O cars from 11 November 1896. Following five sample cars from Milnes, Brush and North Metropolitan, 135 were built by Brown Marshalls, 80 by Midland Railway Carriage & Wagon, 115 by Metropolitan Railway Carriage and Wagon and 29 in the Corporation Works at Coplawhill. All were open top, double-deck uncanopied. 120 were converted for electric traction.

Glasgow Corporation Tramways

134.75 miles, 4ft. 7¾in. gauge. Opened 13 October 1898, closed 1 September 1962. Special service Anderston Cross to Auchenshuggle until 6 September 1962. Livery cadium yellow and green. Route colours, blue, green, red, white and yellow used until circa 1945. Services 2, 5, 7, 10, 12 and 13 wholly or partially replaced by trolleybuses which operated from 3 April 1949 until 27 May 1967.

Car Numbers	Type (as built)	Year built	Builder	Seats	Truck(s)	Motors	Controllers
665-685 (a)	Single-deck Two comp't.	1898	GCT	36	Metropolitan Eqw.bogies	Westinghouse 39B 2 x 35hp	Westinghouse 90
686-687 (b)	Open top Short canopy	1898	GCT	25/30	Brill 21E	Westinghouse 49B 2 x 30hp	Westinghouse 90
688-900 (b)	Open top Short canopy	1899 -1900	GCT	25/30	Brill 21E	Westinghouse 49B 2 x 30hp	BTH B18
901-980 (b)	Open top Short canopy	1900	GRC&W	25/30	Brill 21E	Westinghouse 49B 2 x 30hp	BTH B18
981-1000 (b)	Open top Short canopy	1900 -1901	GCT	25/30	Brill 21E	Westinghouse 49B 2 x 30hp	BTH B18
1-120 (c)	Open top Short canopy	1899 -1903	GCT	18/32	Brill 21E	Westinghouse 49B 2 x 30hp	Westinghouse 210
664-440 665(ii) (b)	Open top Short canopy	1900 -1904	GCT	25/30	Brill 21E	Westinghouse 49B 2 x 30hp	BTH B18
439-337 (d, e)	Balcony	1904 -1906	GCT	24/38'	Brill 21E	Westinghouse 49B 2 x 30hp	BTH B18

Glasgow Corporation Tramways (continued)

Car Numbers	Type (as built)	Year built	Builder	Seats	Truck(s)	Motors	Controllers
336-317 (d)	Balcony	1908	GCT	24/38	Brill 21E	Westinghouse 49B 2 x 30hp	BTH B18
316-287 (b)	Open top Short canopy	1909	GCT	25/30	Brill 21E	Westinghouse 49B 2 x 30hp	BTH B18
286-121 (f)	Balcony	1911 -1919	GCT	24/38	Brill 21E	Westinghouse 49B 2 x 30hp	BTH B18
120-93(ii) (f)	Balcony	1919 -1923	GCT	24/38	Brill 21E	Westinghouse 200 2 x 30hp	BTH B18
91-1(ii) (f)	Balcony	1920 -1923	GCT	24/38	Brill 21E	Westinghouse 323V 2 x 45hp	BTH B18
666-685 (ii) 987 (f)	Balcony	1919 -1924	GCT	24/38	Brill 21E	Westinghouse 323V 2 x 45hp	BTH B18
1039-1040 665(iii) (f)	Balcony	1923 -1929	GCT	24/38	Brill 21E	Westinghouse 323V 2 x 45hp	BTH B18
1050-1051 1088 (f)	Balcony	1924	GCT	24/38	Brlll 21E	Westinghouse 323V 2 x 45hp	BTH B18
1001-1038 1041-1049 (g)	Open top	Bought 1923	BEC	22/33	Brush AA	GE58 6T 2 x 30hp	BTH B18
1052-1072 (h)	Open top	Bought 1923	HN or Brush	24/35	HN or Brush 21E	GEC WT28 or MV101DR 2 x 60hp	BTH B18
1073-1087 (i)	Open top	Bought 1922	Brush	22/34	Brush AA	Brush 1002 2 x 30hp	Brush H2 or HD2
1089 (j)	Single-deck	1926	GCT	36	Brill 77E1 MxT bogies	BTH 264A 4 x 25hp	MV T4A
142(ii) 1090 (k)	Enclosed	1927	GCT	28/40	HN MxT bogies	MV101DR 2 x 60hp	MV OK23B
1091-1120 (k)	Enclosed	1928 -1929	HN	30/38	Kllmarnock MxT bogies	EE DK105 2 x 60hp	EE CD/B2E
1121-1130 (k)	Enclosed	1928 -1929	RYP	30/38	Kilmarnock MxT bogies	GEC WT28 2 x 60hp	MV OK 26B
1131-1140 (k)	Enclosed	1928 -1929	Brush	30/38	Kilmarnock MxT bogies	EE DK105 2 x 60hp	MV OK26B
1141-1142 (l)	Enclosed	1936 -1937	GCT	27/38	EMB or M&T EqW bogies	MV 109AW 4 x 35hp	MV EP
1143-1292 (m)	Enclosed	1937 -1941	GCT	26/38	EMB Eqw or LtW bogies	BTH 109AW 4 x 35hp	BTH EP
1001(ii)	Enclosed	1939	GCT	24/38	M&T 588	MV 101DR 2 x 60hp	MV OK26B
1002(ii)	Enclosed	1939	GCT	24/36	M&T 588	CP C162BB 2 x 70hp	CP EP
1003-1004 (ii) (n)	Enclosed	1940	GCT	24/36	EMB Flexible axle	GEC WT28 2 x 60hp	MV OK26B
6(iii)	Enclosed	1943	GCT	24/36	Brush 21E	MV 101DR 2 x 60hp	MV OK26B
1005(ii) (o)	Enclosed	1947	GCT	34/38	M&T HS44 EqW. bogies	CP 90A-10 4 x 45hp	CP CT/MM1
1293-1392 (p)	Enclosed	1948 -1952	GCT	30/40 26/40	M&T 596 EqW bogies	MV 109AR 4 x 36hp	MV EP
1006-1016 1018-1038(ii) (q)	Enclosed	Bought 1953 -1954	LCT	34/44	M&T Swing-linkbogies	GEC WT184 4 x 35hp	CP EP
1041-1049 1052-1056(ii) (q)	Enclosed	Bought 1954	LCT	34/44	EMB LtW or HyW bogies	GEC WT184 4 x 35hp	CP-EP
1393-1398 (r)	Enclosed	1954	GCT	26/38	EMB LtW bogies	GEC WT 184 4 x 35h p	MV EP

Notes

(a) Known as 'Room & Kitchen' or 'But & Ben' cars. No. 672 preserved. No. 671 and one other purchased by the Paisley Company and used as tea rooms at Rouken Glen.

(b) Standard 'Round dash' (Phase 1) cars. No. 687 originally had a Peckham Cantilever truck. Some cars had Witting motors, others Westinghouse 90M or Type 210 controllers. Many of the original motors were replaced by 45hp Westinghouse 323V's. No. 729 was the Motor School car and did not enter public service until 1924.
All, except No. 987, were modernised over the years, top-covered, and by 1935 totally enclosed, seating 21/38, on Brush 21E or M&G 21E trucks with 60hp MV 101DR, EE DK105, GEC WT28 or BTH 506A motors. MV OK20B, MV OK 23B, MV OK 26B, BTH OK45B or EE CD2 controllers were fitted. Nine cars fitted EMB Flexible axle trucks latterly.

Glasgow Corporation Tramways (Notes continued)

(c) Electrified horse cars. The majority of cars from No. 50 onwards had 35hp Witting motors and BTH B18 controllers. A few 35hp BTH GE58 motors. Five cars had BTH B13 controllers. No. 92 converted to single-deck one-man car seating 24.
Nos. 24, 32, 47 and 116 sold to Dumbarton; No.118 to Luton.

(d) Standard 'Round dash' (phase 2) cars. Controllers as note b. All modernised, 1928-1935, as note b.

(e) Nos. 437-338 initially seated 24/42.

(f) Standard 'Hex dash' (phase 3). Majority of cars built post 1915 had 45hp Westinghouse 220 motors, and post 1918 Type 323V. Modernised as note b. Nos.15 and 142 were lengthened and mounted on Brill 39E1 and LCC MxT bogies respectively.

(g) Ex-Paisley Nos. 1-38, 41-49 built 1904-5. Nos. 9-19, 22-24, 27, 37-38 cut down to single-deck for Duntocher service 1924-5. No. 1008 illuminated car, No. 1017 School car. Paisley Nos. 39-40 were not renumbered.

(h) Ex-Paisley Nos. 52-72 built 1907-20. Modernised as note b above, 1924-31, on Brush 21E trucks and fitted 60hp GEC WT28 or 45hp MV101DR motors. MV OK26B or EE CDB2 controllers.

(i) Ex-Airdrie and Coatbridge Nos. 1-15. Nos. 13-15 top covered when acquired. No. 1078 fitted Brill 21E truck, Nos. 1084-87 fitted Brill 21E trucks and Westinghouse B49 motors, No. 1083 GE58 motors and No. 1084 Brill 21E truck and GE58 motors. No.1073 converted to an illuminated car.

(j) Experimental single-deck car.

(k) 'Kilmarnock Bogies'. The motors, 60hp EE DK105, GEC WT28 and MV 101DR, were used indiscriminately on these cars. The body of No.1100 was modified. Nos. 142(ii), 1090 were prototypes.

(l) Prototype 'Coronation' cars. No. 1141 had EMB L5 bogies; No. 1142 had Maley & Taunton Swing-link type.

(m) 'Coronation' cars.

(n) No. 1004 had GEC 60hp WR283 motors and GEC remote control equipment.

(o) Initially single-ended. Converted in 1956 to 'Cunarder' design.

(p) 'Cunarder' cars. Later cars seated 26 in the saloon.

(q) Ex-Liverpool Nos. 869, 871, 874-5, 877-8, 880-1, 883-7, 890-1, 893, 897, 899, 901-4, 918-9, 921-42 built 1936-37. Nos.1031-36, 1038 EMB lightweight; 1039 EMB heavyweight bogies.

(r) Coronation design bogies ex-Liverpool Corporation Tramways.

Works cars

There were initially three separately numbered series of cars. They were four mains testing cars, nine permanent way cars and nine water cars. They were renumbered in the 1920's as follows:

Car numbers	Type	Date built	Builder	Truck(s)	Motors	Controllers
No. 1 (a)	Mains Dept.	1905	GCT	Brill 21E	GE 58 2 x 30hp	BTH B18
No. 2 (b)	Mains Dept. Tool Van	1912	GCT	Brill 21E	Westinghouse 49B 2 x 30hp	BTH B18
No. 3 (c)	Mains Dept.	1908	GCT	GCT Eq.W bogies	Westinghouse 49B 2 x 35hp	BTH B18
No. 3-No. 10 (d)	Sand-Sett wagons	1906 -1920	GCT	GCT Eq.W bogies	Westinghouse 49B 2 x 30hp	Westinghouse 90
No.11-No.19 (e)	Water cars	1907	GCT	Brill 21E or M&G 21EM	Various 2 x 30hp	Various
No. 20 (f)	Mains Dept. Tool Van	1903	GCT	Brill 21E	GE58? 2 x 30hp	BTH B18?
No. 20(ii) (g)	Mains Dept. Tool Van	1925	GCT	Brush AA	GE58 2 x 30hp	BTH B13
No. 21-No. 22 (h)	PW Dept. Tool Van	1903 -1906	GCT	Brill 21E	GE58 2 x 30hp	BTH B18
No. 22(ii) (i)	PW Dept. Tool Van	1938	GCT	Brill 21E	Westinghouse 323V 2 x 45hp	BTH B18
No. 23 (j)	PW Dept Tool Van	1952	GCT	Brush 21E	Westinghouse 220 2 x 45hp	BTH B18
No. 23A (k)	PW Dept Tool Van	1938	GCT	Brill 21E	BTH 101J 2 x 60hp	BTH OK49B
No. 24 (l)	Overhead Dept.	1924	GCT	Brush 21E	Brush 1002 2 x 30hp	Brush?
No. 25 (m)	Mineral Wagon	1924	GCT	HN 21E	GE58 2 x 30hp	BTH B18
No. 26-No. 32 (n)	Tool van	1933 -1934	GCT	Brush AA Brill 21E	GE 58 2 x 30hp	BTH B18
No. 33-No. 37 (o)	Sett wagon	1937	GCT	Brill 21E	Westinghouse 323V 2 x 45hp	BTH B18
No. 38-No. 39 (p)	Sand wagon	1939	GCT	Brill 21E	Westinghouse 323V 2 x 45hp	BTH B18
No. 40 (q)	Tool van	1954	GCT	Brush 21E	BTH 101J 2 x 60hp	BTH OK49B
No. 50 (r)	Illuminated car	c1930	GCT	Brush 21E	GEC 2 x 60hp	EE CDB2 ?
No. 51	Sand/Sett wagon	1907	HN	HN 21E	GE58 2 x 30hp	BTH B18
No. 101 (s)	Water car	1906	Brush	Brush AA	GE58 2 x 30hp	BTH B18

The trucks, motors and controllers are those with which the cars entered service with the PW Department.

Tool Car No. 30 was adapted from ex-Paisley No. 1026. Seen in Barrland Street PW Yard on 7 August 1954. The suburban Lines from Glasgow Central passed alongside the yard. *(R. J. S. Wiseman*

Glasgow Corporation (continued)

(a)   Cable laying car. Now at the National Tramway Museum.
(b)   Converted horse car No. 120.
(c)   Ex-Single-deck No. 672. Mains Testing Car.
(d)   No. 9 Decorated car 'Queen Mary' 1937.
(e)   Motors included Westinghouse 49B, 220, and 323V; GE 58 and GE203L. Controllers included Westinghouse 90 and BTH B18.
      In 1951 No. 14 fitted 60hp BTH 101J motors and MV OK45B controllers.
      The majority of the cars following were similarly re-equipped.
(f)   May have been converted horse car No. 120.
(g)   Ex-Paisley No. 39. Later fitted 30hp Westinghouse 49B motors and BTH B18 controllers.
(h)   Tool vans. No. 22 converted horse car No. 31 and fitted 30hp Westinghouse 49B motors. No. 21 at the National Tramway Museum.
(i)   Later fitted GCT/Brush 21E truck. Sold to the National Tramway Museum for parts, the truck to Glasgow Standard 22.
(j)   Ex-No. 814. Originally numbered 23B.
(k)   Later fitted with 45hp Westinghouse 323V motors.
(l)   Ex-Airdrie and Coatbridge open top car. Overhead Inspection car.
(m)   Truck and equipment ex-Paisley 40.
(n)   Ex-Paisley. Nos. 1021, 1005, 1003, 1007, 1026, 1004, 1002 respectively.
(o)   Trucks of Nos. 34-37 ex-756, 906, 771 and 791 respectively.
(p)   Conveyed dry sand to the various depots.
(q)   Ex-No. 722.
(r)   Ex-Paisley works car No. 51 rebuilt by GCT.
(s)   Ex-Paisley No. 50. Later fitted 45hp Westinghouse 323V motors. Sold to Tramway Museum Society for parts.

Kinlochleven Aluminium Works

1.25 miles, 3ft. 0in. gauge. Opened 1908 Closed 1959.

Locomotive number	Type	Year built	Builder	Truck(s)	Motors	Controllers
1-2	Bo	1908	Dick Kerr	5ft. 6in.	DK 2 x 35hp	DK DB1? Form C
3	Bo	1947	Metrovick	5ft. 6in.	MV 2 x 35hp	MV OK 35B

Greenock & Port Glasgow Tramways Company

7.42 miles, 4ft. 7¾in. gauge. Opened 3 October 1901, closed 15 July 1929. Livery dark red and white.

The Company operated horse tramways from 29 November 1889 until 7 November 1901 with a fleet of open top cars built in 1889 by Milnes and six cars ex-Vale of Clyde Tramways.

Car Numbers	Type (as built)	Year Built	Builder	Seats	Truck(s)	Motors	Controllers
1-30 (a)	Open top	1901	Brush	30/44	Brush B MxT bogie	Brush 1000A 2 x 25hp?	Brush
31-36 (b)	Single-deck Combination	1904	Brush	30	Brush Conaty	Brush	Brush
37-39 (c)	Open top	1906	Brush	22/36	Brush Conaty	Brush	Brush
40 (d)	Single-deck Demi car	1908	UEC	20	Brill 21E	Westinghouse	Raworth
41-43 (e)	Balcony	1911	Brush	22/36	Brush	Brush	Brush
44-46	Open top	1916	Brush	18/30	Brush	—	—
47-48 (f)	Single-deck Combination	Bought 1915	ER&TCW	46	Brush B MxT bogies	Brush	Brush
—	Water car	1901	Brush	—	Brush A	Brush ?	Brush ?

Notes

(a) Nos. 10 (or 11) and 27 later fitted balcony covers seating 30/48
(b) Conaty & Lycett Radial trucks. Rebuilt 1906 as open top cars seating 24/26. Nos. 35, 36 later fitted balcony covers seating 24/28.
(c) Conaty & Lycett radial trucks.
(d) Body only transferred to Rothesay c1924.
(e) Trailers. Fleet numbers not verified.
(f) Built 1902, Rothesay Tramways series Nos. 11-15. Greenock fleet numbers not verified.

Lanarkshire Tramways Company

28.43 miles, 4ft. 7¾in. gauge. Opened 22 July 1903, closed 14 February 1931. Livery dark green and white. Opened as the Hamilton, Motherwell and Wishaw Light Railways Company with cars Nos.1-25 in a livery of light blue and off-white.

Car numbers	Type (as built)	Year built	Builder	Seats	Truck(s)	Motors	Controllers
1-25 (a)	Open top	1903	BEC	24/32	BEC SC60	GE58-6T 2 x 27hp	BTH B18
26-46 (b)	Open top	1904-6	Brush	24/35	Brush AA	GE58-6T 2 x 27hp	BTH B18
47-53 (c)	Open top	1908	UEC	24/35	M&G 21EM	GE58-6T 2 x 27hp	BTH B18
54-60 (d)	Open top	1909	Brush	24/35	Brush Flexible-axle	GE58-6T 2 x 27hp	BTH B18
61-76 (e)	Open top	1911-3	Brush	24/35	M&G 21EM	GE58-6T 2 x 27hp	BTH B18
77 (f)	Balcony	1924	LTC	26/42	HN 21E	BTH 265J 2 x 40hp	BTH B510
45, 54, 56 (ii) (g)	Balcony	1925	LTC	26/42	HN 21E	BTH 265J 2 x 40hp	BTH B510
78-89 (g)	Balcony	1925	HN	26/42	HN 21E	BTH 265J 2 x 40hp	BTH B510
—	Works car	1903	McGuire	—	Brush	GE	BTH B18

Notes

(a) A Type. All reconstructed, bodies in the Company workshops and the trucks by Hurst Nelson, 1912-1923.
(b) B Type. Bodies reconstructed in the Company workshops, 1920-24. K Type.
(c) C Type Bodies reconstructed in the Company workshops, 1921-22. M Type.
(d) B Type Bodies reconstructed in the Company workshops, 1921-24.
    No.60 rebuilt as a front-exit car in 1924.
(e) D Type
(f) N Type Prototype low-bridge car with front entrance.
(g) N Type

Ten BTH265J motors were sold to Blackburn and six Hurst Nelson trucks to South Shields in 1932.

Kilmarnock Corporation Tramways

4.24 miles, 4ft. 8½in. gauge. Opened 10 December 1904, closed 3 May 1926. Livery olive green and cream.

Car numbers	Type (as built)	Year built	Builder	Seats	Truck(s)	Motors	Controllers
1-11 (a)	Open top	1904	HN	22/30	HN Pressed steel	Witting 2 x 25hp	Witting
12 (b)	Open top	1905	HN	22/30	HN 21E	Witting 2 x 25hp	BTH B18?
13-14 (c)	Balcony	1905	HN	24/32	HN 21E	Witting 2 x 25hp	BTH B18?

Notes

(a)   The Witting Eborall equipments were made by the Société l'Electrique et l'Hydraulique of Charleroi, Belgium. Later Ateliers de Constructions Electriques de Charleroi.
(b)   The Hurst Nelson Exhibition Car at London 1905.
(c)   The trucks from Nos. 13-14 sold to Ayr and fitted to Nos. 11-12.

Paisley Tramways Company Ltd.

2.44 miles, 4ft.7¾in. gauge. Opened 30 December 1885, closed 21 November 1903. Livery red and white.

Rolling stock initially comprised five double-deck, open top, and two single-deck cars built by the Glasgow Tramways & Omnibus Company. In 1890 two more single-deck cars were added and two of the original cars rebuilt. On closure there were eight cars, four single-deck, including two ex-Glasgow Corporation Tramways, and four double-deck.

Paisley District Tramways Company

18.23 miles, 4ft. 7¾in. gauge. Opened 13 June 1904, transferred to Glasgow Corporation, 1 August 1923. Closed 11 May 1957. Livery red and off-white.

Car numbers	Type (as built)	Year built	Builder	Seats	Truck(s)	Motors	Controllers
1-39	Open top	1904	BEC	22/33	Brush AA	GE58-6T 2 x 30hp	BTH B18
40-49	Open top	1905	BEC	22/33	Brush AA	GE58-6T 2 x 30hp	BTH B18
50	Water car	1906	Brush	—	Brush AA	GE58-6T 2 x 30hp	BTH B18
51	PW car	1907	HN	—	HN Solid -forged	GE58-6T 2 x 30hp	BTH B18
52 (a)	Open top	1907	HN	22/33	HN Solid -forged	GE58-6T 2 x 30hp	BTH B18
53-58 (b)	Balcony	1911	HN	24/35	HN Swing -bolster	GE58-6T 2 x 30hp	BTH B18
59-62	Open top	1912	Brush	24/35	Brush AA	GE58-6T 2 x 30hp	BTH B18
53-58 (ii)	Open top	1915	Brush	24/35	Brush 21E	GE58-6T 2 s 30hp	BTH B18
63-67	Open top	1916	HN	24/35	HN Solid -forged	GE200K 2 x 40hp	BTH B49
68-72	Open top	1920	HN	24/35	HN Solid -forged	GE200K 2 x 40hp	BTH B49
— (c)	Single-deck	Bought 1920	SCT	28	Brill 21E	BTH GE58 2 x 35hp	BTH B13

Notes

(a)   Hurst Nelson top cover fitted in 1910.
(b)   Similar to the LCC 'M' class. Sold to Dundee in 1914.
(c)   Sheffield 202 built in 1903. No evidence of the car being renumbered in the Paisley fleet or being used in service.
There were also four open wagons built on individual bogies from Glasgow Corporation single-deck cars Nos. 666-685 of 1898.

Rothesay Tramways Company Ltd.

2.37 miles, 4ft. 0in. gauge. Horse traction. Opened 10 June 1882, closed 2 March 1902. Also from 17 May 1902 until 19 August 1902 on 3ft 6in gauge tracks. Livery latterly maroon and cream.

Initially twelve single-deck cars were supplied by the Savile Street Foundry of Sheffield — Nos. 1-8 open seating 32 passengers, and Nos. 9-12 closed seating 20 passengers. Further open cars were built locally; Nos. 13-14 by James McBride and Nos. 15-19 by William Lauder.

Rothesay Tramways Company Ltd.

4.81 miles, 3ft. 6in. gauge. Opened 19 August 1902, closed 30 September 1936. Livery red and white; from 1931 blue and cream.

Car numbers	Type (as built)	Year built	Builder	Seats	Truck(s)	Motors	Controllers
1-10 (a)	Single-deck	1902	ER&TCW	32+18	Brill 22E RMxT bogies	DK 25B 2 x 25hp	DK DB1 Form B
11-15 (b)	Single-deck Combination	1902	ER&TCW	46	Brill 22E MxT bogies	DK 25B 2 x 25hp	DK DB1 Form B
16-20 (a)	Single-deck	1903	Brush	46	Brush EqW bogies	Brush 1000B 2 x 25hp	Brush HD2
21 (c)	Demi car	Bought 1924	UEC	20	Brill 21E	Westinghouse	Raworth
22 (d)	Single-deck	1928	RTC	45	Brill 21E	Westinghouse	Westinghouse

Notes

(a) Crossbench car with end saloons.
(b) Open end compartments. Bodies of Nos. 11-12 sold to Greenock c1916. Nos. 11-12 then rebuilt as open toastracks c1920 on the 22E Maximum traction bogies. Seating 80 on 16 benches.
(c) Built 1908 for Greenock & Port Glasgow Company.
(d) Open crossbench car built on the frame and truck of No. 21.

Summerlee Heritage Park

0.5 miles, 4ft. 8½in. gauge. Opened 1 April 1988.

Car numbers	Type (as built)	Year built	Builder	Seats	Truck(s)	Motors	Controllers
53 (a)	Open top	1908	UEC	24/35	Brill 21E	GE 2 x 55hp	B-54 Type C
225 (b)	Single-deck Saloon	1949	SGP	16	?	?	?
392 (c)	Single-deck	1951	Duewag	10	?	?	?
1016 (d)	Single-deck	1904	BEC	24	Brill 21E	?	EE DB1
1017 (e)	Single-deck	1904	BEC	20	Brill 21E	?	EE DB1
1245 (f)	Enclosed	1939	GCT	26/38	EMB bogies	BTH 109AW 4 x 35hp	BTH
9062 (g)	Single-deck	1959	STIB	17	Brill 79E	MTV 20	ACEC
— (h)	Open top	1894	Midland	?	—	—	—

Notes

(a) Rebuilt as Type M from the lower saloons of two Lanarkshire cars. Equipment from Oporto No. 150.
(b) Ex-Graz.
(c) Ex-Dusseldorf. Adapted for wheelchair use.
(d) Ex-Paisley 16, Glasgow 1016. Stored, not owned by Summerlee.
(e) Ex-Paisley 17, Restored 2002 as Glasgow 1017. School Car.
(f) Glasgow Coronation owned by North Lanarkshire Council. Stored elsewhere pending restoration for ultimate display at Summerlee.
(g) Rebuild of Brussels 4062 in 1959.
(h) Ex-Leamington & Warwick horse tram which may have originated with Glasgow Corporation. Number not known. Under restoration.

Vale of Clyde Tramways Company — Govan Section

2.25 miles, 4ft. 7¾in. Horse traction from 16 December 1872, steam traction authorised from 21 July 1877, but not used until some weeks later. Steam traction ceased on 9 July 1893. Then horse operation leased by the Glasgow Tramway & Omnibus Company until 11 November 1896 and finally by Glasgow Corporation until 9 August 1901. Livery brown and cream.

Locomotives:- Nos. 1-10 Hughes, 1877, Nos. 1-9(ii), Kitson, 1881, No. 10(ii) Kitson, ex-Cavehill & Whitewell Tramways Company.
Trailers:- Nos. 1-12, 1872, double-deck knifeboard, Nos. 1-8(ii), 1881, double-deck knifeboard by Metropolitan, seating 30/30. Nos. 9-10(ii), 1883, seating 32/32. The above steam rolling stock was hired from Hughes and Kitson.

Vale of Clyde Tramways Company — Greenock Section

4.5 miles, 4ft. 7¾in. gauge. Horse traction. Opened 7 July 1873. Transferred to Greenock Company on 7 July 1894. Livery brown and cream.

Trailers:- Nos. 1-12, 1873; Nos.13-14, 1875-76, double-deck, knifeboard by Tramway Car & Works Company, Glasgow. Some used initially on the Govan section.

Key to abbreviations and manufacturers

Ashhury	—	The Ashbury Railway Carriage and Iron Co. Ltd., Manchester.
BEC	—	The British Electric Car Co. Ltd., Trafford Park, Manchester.
Brill	—	The J. G. Brill Company, Inc., Philadelphia, USA
Brown Marshalls	—	Brown Marshall & Co., Ltd., Adderley Park, Birmingham.
Brush	—	The Brush Electrical Engineering Co. Ltd., Loughborough.
BTH	—	The British Thomson-Houston Company Ltd., Rugby.
Conaty	—	Conaty & Lycett Radial trucks, built by Brush except one or two experimental models.
CP	—	Crompton Parkinson Ltd., Traction Division, Chelmsford.
Duewag	—	Waggonfabrik Uerdingen Werk, Dusseldorf.
DK	—	Dick, Kerr & Co. Ltd., Preston. Lancashire.
E & H	—	Société l'Electrique et l'Hydraulique, Charleroi, Belgium. (Later ACEC)
EE	—	English Electric Co. Ltd., Preston, Lancashire.
EMB	—	The Electro-Mechanical Brake Co.Ltd., West Bromwich, Staffs.
EP	—	Electro-pneumatic control.
Eq.W	—	Equal-wheel bogies.
ER&TCW	—	The Electric Railway & Tramway Carriage Works Ltd. Preston.
GRC&W	—	Gloucester Railway Carriage & Wagon Co., Ltd., Gloucester.
GCT	—	Glasgow Corporation Tramways, Coplawhill Works.
GE	—	The General Electric Company Inc. Schenectady, NY, USA.
GEC	—	General Electric Co. Ltd., Witton Works, Birmingham.
GT & O	—	Glasgow Tramway & Omnibus Co. Ltd., Crown Point Works, Glasgow.
HN	—	Hurst Nelson & Company Ltd., Motherwell, Scotland.
Hughes	—	Henry Hughes & Co., Falcon Works, Loughborough.
HyW	—	Heavyweight bogies.
Kitson	—	Kitson & Co. Ltd., Airedale Foundary, Leeds.
Lancaster	—	Lancaster Railway Carriage and Wagon Co. Ltd. Caton Rd. Lancaster
LCT	—	Liverpool Corporation Transport, Edge Lane Works, Liverpool.
LCCT	—	London County Council Tramways, Charlton Works.
LtW	—	Lightweight bogies.
LTC	—	Lanarkshire Tramways Company, Motherwell, Scotland.
MCT	—	Manchester Corporation Tramways, Hyde Road Works.
McGuire	—	McGuire Manufacturing Co., Ltd., Bury, Lancashire.
Metropolitan	—	Metropolitan Railway Carriage & Wagon Co., Ltd., Saltley, Birmingham.
Midland	—	Midland Railway Carriage & Wagon Co., Ltd, Shrewsbury, later Birmingham.
Milnes	—	G. F. Milnes & Co. Ltd., Hadley, Shropshire.(also at Birkenhead).
M & G	—	Mountain & Gibson Ltd., Bury, Lancashire.
M & T	—	Maley & Taunton Ltd. Wednesbury, Staffordshire.
MV	—	Metropolitan Vickers Electrical Co. Ltd. Trafford Park, Manchester.
MxT	—	Maximum Traction bogies.
North Metropolitan	—	North Metropolitan Tramways Co., Leytonstone, Essex.
Peckham	—	Peckham Truck & Engineering Co., Ltd.
Raworth	—	Raworth's Traction Patents Ltd., Manchester.
RMxT	—	Reversed Maximum Traction bogies.
RYP	—	R. Y. Pickering & Co., Ltd., Wishaw, Lanarkshire.
SCT	—	Sheffield Corporation Tramways, Queens Road Works.
SGP	—	Semmering, Graz, Pauker Werk, Graz, Austria.
Starbuck	—	Starbuck Car & Wagon Co. Ltd., Birkenhead.
Stephenson	—	Stephenson Carriage & Wagon Co., New York, USA.
STIB	—	Société des Transports Intercommuneaux de Bruxelles.
Westinghouse	—	Westinghouse Electric Co. Ltd. Trafford Park, Manchester.
Witting	—	Witting, Eborall & Co. Ltd., Westminster, London.

The Electric Railway & Tramway Carriage Works Ltd. (renamed United Electric Car Company Ltd. from 25 September 1905) was a subsidiary of Dick, Kerr & Co. ltd. which merged with other electrical companies on 14 December 1918 to form the English Electric Company Ltd. The Company also had works at Bradford, Rugby and Stafford. Most post-1908 Peckham trucks were made by the Brush Electrical Engineering Co.Ltd., and also by HN, EE and EMB. Metropolitan-Vickers were successors to British Westinghouse.

Acknowledgements and Sources

This book is based on Chapter 12 of *Great British Tramway Networks* by W. H. Bett and J. C. Gillham (Fourth Edition, LRTL 1962) with additional information from recent books and articles, especially *The Glasgow Tramcar* by Ian G. McM. Stewart, and the various books on the Scottish systems published by NB Traction over several years. Periodicals consulted have included *The BET Gazette*, *Light Railway and Tramway Journal*, *Modern Tramway*, *Modern Transport*, *Railway Magazine*, *Scottish Tramlines*, *Scottish Transport*, *The Tramway and Railway World* and *Tramway Review*.

Thanks are due to Rosie Thacker, Librarian, and Glynn Wilton, Photographic Officer, at the National Tramway Museum for their help with source material and for locating photographs. Thanks are also due to A. W. Brotchie, D. S. Brown, I. A. Souter, Ian G. McM. Stewart, W. Tuckwell and the late J.H.Price.

The tramcar fleet lists have been compiled by R. J. S. Wiseman with the valued assistance of A. W. Brotchie, B. Longworth, S. J. T. Robertson, Ian G. McM. Stewart, and W. Tuckwell. The publishers will be pleased to receive any additional information and this will be published in *Tramway Review*. The maps have been drawn by R. A. Smith and are based on information on those originally drawn by J. C. Gillham and D. L. Thomson for Glasgow, with additional input from D. S. Brown and B. Longworth. Those for Airdrie, Ayr, Dumbarton, Kilmarnock and Paisley on those by A. W. Brotchie. The map of Greenock is based on the Ordnance Survey edition of 1914, and that of Ardrossan on the plans held in The National Archives of Scotland in Edinburgh. The area map is based on that by J. C. Gillham.

Photographs have been reproduced by kind permission of Ayr Carnegie Library, R. W. Brash, Roy Brook, A. W. Brotchie, North Lanarkshire Council Community Resources, Science Museum, Science and Society Picture Library, London, South Lanarkshire Council, The Royal Scottish Museum, Ian Stewart, The Tramway Museum Society and M.G.C.W Wheeler.

Bibliography — General
Great British Tramway Networks, by W. H. Bett and J. C. Gillham. (Light Railway Transport League, 4th. Edition, 1962).
Scottish Tramway Fleets, by A. W. Brotchie, (N.B.Traction, 1968).
The Definitive Guide to Trams (including funiculars) in the British Isles, by David Voice, (Adam Gordon, 2001).
What Colour Was That Tram? by David Voice, (Author 4th. Edition, 1998).

Airdrie
Tramways of the Monklands, by I. L.Cormack, (Scottish Tramway Museum Society, 1964).
Airdrie and Coatbridge Tramways, by I. L. Cormack, (in *Lanarkshire's Trams* N.B.Traction, 1993).

Ardrossan and Largs
Green Cars to Hurlford by Brian T. Deans, (Scottish Tramway Museum Society, 1986).

Ayr
The Tramways of Ayr, by Ronald W. Brash, (N.B.Traction, 1983).

Opposite: FULL SPEED AHEAD — Down the Renfrew Road. The Andrew Barclay 0-4-0 Saddle tank en-route from Stephen's Linthouse Yard to Shieldhall Goods Yard.
(M. G. C. W. Wheeler

Carstairs

The Carstairs Electric Light Railway, (in Chambers Journal, 22 June 1895).
Carstairs House Tramway by A. W. Brotchie, (in *Lanarkshire's Trams*),

Dumbarton

A Tram Ride to Loch Lomond, by James Campbell (in *Scottish Transport, No.23, 1973*).
Dumbarton's Trams and Buses by A. W. Brotchie and R. L. Grieves, (N.B.Traction, 1985).

Glasgow

The Glasgow Tramcar, by Ian G. McM. Stewart, (Scottish Tramway and Transport Society, 1994).
A Handbook of Glasgow Tramways, by D. L. Thomson, (Scottish Tramway Museum Society, 1961).
The Glasgow Horse Tramways by Struan Jno. T. Robertson, (Scottish Tramway and Transport Society, 2000).
Glasgow Garden Festival by Brian T. Deans and Ian Stewart (in *Scottish Transport* Nos. 43-44, 1987, 1988).

Govan

The Govan Burgh Tramways by M. Morton Hunter, (in *Scottish Transport, No.27, 1975*)

Greenock

Greenock and Port Glasgow Tramways Co., by I. L. Coonie, (in *Scottish Transport*, No.26, 1975).
The Tramways of Greenock, Gourock and Port Glasgow, by I. L. Cormack, (Scottish Tramway Museum Society, 1976).

Kilmarnock

Kilmarnock's Trams and Buses, by A. W. Brotchie and R. L. Grieves, (N.B.Traction 1984).
Green Cars to Hurlford, by Brian T. Deans, (Scottish Tramway Museum Society, 1986).

Motherwell

Lanarkshire Tramways Company by I. L. Cormack and A. W. Brotchie. (in *Lanarkshire's Trams*, N.B.Traction, 1993).

Paisley

Paisley's Trams and Buses, Eighties to Twenties, by A. W. Brotchie and R. L. Grieves, (N.B.Traction, 1986).
Paisley's Trams and Buses, Twenties to Eighties, by A. W. Brotchie and R. L. Grieves, (N.B.Traction, 1988).

Rothesay

The Tramways of Rothesay, by I. L. Cormack, (Scottish Tramway and Transport Society, 1995).

Summerlee, Coatbridge

Summerlee's Tramway by A. Harper, (in Lanarkshire's Trams, N.B.Traction,1993).

Inside back cover

Above **Summerlee Museum, Coatbridge. Restored Lanarkshire tramcar No.53 decorated for its inauguration on 1 April 1995.** *(R. J. S. Wiseman*

Below **"The Lanarkshire Tramways Co. beg to draw attention to the advantages of sending parcels by the Company's Parcel Delivery Service on the line of routes. Low rates. Prompt Delivery." So reads the back of this postcard.** *(Electrical Press Ltd,, courtesy A. W. Brotchie*

Published by the Light Rail Transit Association, 13A The Precinct, Broxbourne, Herts. EN10 7HY
Printed by W. J. Ray, Spectrum House, Leamore Lane, Walsall WS2 7DQ. Tel: (01922) 428267